AXELROD & COOPER'S CONCISE GUIDE TO WRITING

Instructor's Resource Manual

AXELROD & COOPER'S CONCISE GUIDE TO WRITING

Third Edition

Rise B. Axelrod
UNIVERSITY OF CALIFORNIA, RIVERSIDE

Charles R. Cooper
UNIVERSITY OF CALIFORNIA, SAN DIEGO

Lenora Penna Smith

Alison M. Warriner
CALIFORNIA STATE UNIVERSITY, HAYWARD

BEDFORD/ST. MARTIN'S

BOSTON ◆ NEW YORK

Manufactured in the United States of America.

6 5 4 3 2
f e d c b a

For information, write: Bedford/St. Martin's, 75 Arlington Street, Boston, MA 02116   (617-399-4000)

ISBN: 0-312-39677-5

Introduction

This *Instructor's Resource Manual* offers a compendium of practical suggestions that will help you and your students have a productive and enjoyable experience working with *Axelrod & Cooper's Concise Guide to Writing*, third edition. The methods we suggest here are ones we have borrowed from others or developed on our own while teaching the assignments in the *Concise Guide*'s "parent" book, *The St. Martin's Guide to Writing*. The manual, which has been reorganized for the *Concise Guide*'s third edition, begins with a section devoted to teaching strategies that will be of greatest benefit to novice instructors. The second section supplies suggested course plans, strategies for teaching the major assignments, and detailed chapter plans that will also be helpful to new instructors. Even if you have taught with previous editions of the *Concise Guide*, you will find much that is new in Part Two of this manual.

The strategies covered in Part One include both teaching and evaluation practices. We begin with a chapter on teaching practices that play a vital role in the composition course, such as holding conferences with students, organizing in-class workshops, having students keep journals, presenting and discussing readings, and setting up collaborative learning groups. The second chapter includes general advice about responding to student writing, assigning portfolios, and responding to error.

Part Two of this *Instructor's Resource Manual* will help you familiarize yourself with the third edition of *Axelrod & Cooper's Concise Guide to Writing*. Chapter 3 gives you a brief overview of the chapters in the students' book and presents two different course plans, one for a fifteen-week semester and one for a ten-week quarter. Chapter 4 takes a general look at the various chapter features that support each of the major writing assignments (Chapters 2 through 7 of the student edition) and how you may use them in the classroom. Chapter 5, the final chapter in this section of the manual, is also the most substantial; it provides detailed plans for teaching every chapter in the *Concise Guide*, including those chapters that this *Instructor's Resource Manual* does not elsewhere elaborate upon (Chapter 1 and Chapters 8 through 14). For Chapters 2 through 7 of the student edition, we focus here on ways of approaching each of the writing assignments. For the other chapters, we briefly outline the structure and provide suggestions for teaching the exercises.

This *Instructor's Resource Manual* concludes with a selected bibliography in rhetoric and composition. You may also wish to visit the book companion site at <www.bedfordstmartins.com/conciseguide> for links to additional resources.

We would be delighted to receive comments and suggestions for future editions from users of the *Concise Guide*. You may contact us care of Bedford/ St. Martin's at 33 Irving Place, New York, NY 10003.

In addition, we always are looking for new student essays for the *Concise Guide* along with *The St. Martin's Guide to Writing* and the accompanying collection of student writing, *Sticks and Stones and other student essays*. Please consider encouraging your students to send us contributions for potential publication. All you need to do is fill out copies of the agreement forms (found both at the back of this *Instructor's Resource Manual* and in the student edition) and send them to the indicated address.

To order *Axelrod & Cooper's Concise Guide to Writing*, third edition, *Sticks and Stones*, fourth edition, or additional copies of this *Instructor's Resource Manual*, contact your local Bedford/St. Martin's sales representative or e-mail sales_support@bfwpub.com.

Rise B. Axelrod
Charles R. Cooper

Contents

Teaching
Practices

1

In this chapter, we discuss ways you can conduct conferences with students, organize in-class workshops, have students keep journals, present and discuss readings, set up collaborative learning groups, and conduct community service learning projects. The methods we suggest here are ones we have borrowed from others or developed on our own while teaching the assignments in the *Concise Guide*'s "parent" book, *The St. Martin's Guide to Writing*.

HOLDING CONFERENCES

Conferences with students are time-consuming and difficult to schedule when classes are large, but we highly recommend them as a teaching practice, even if you can see students individually only once or twice during the course. Conferences may replace class meetings altogether as the forum in which instructor and students meet, and we have successfully used this format for writing courses. Usually, however, we use conferences in addition to class meetings, because the combination allows us the benefits of group discussion of assignments, drafts, and readings, as well as the chance to work closely with each student and attend to his or her individual needs. Conferences allow the instructor to develop a rapport with students, thus building the trust and self-confidence that many students need before they will take the risks in their writing that lead to real progress. For many students, these conferences are their only opportunities to work individually with a college instructor.

A conference may be scheduled at any time during the composing process. We find a conference most useful after the first or second draft of an essay has been written, at a point when the student has spent some time thinking about the assignment, generating invention notes, and making at least one attempt to put the ideas into draft form but before he or she has finished work on the essay. Ideally, the first draft is discussed in a conference and the second draft in a workshop with other students, or vice versa, before the student writes the final revision of the essay. We do not discuss finished essays in conferences; the time is just too valuable to spend it justifying our remarks on the revision of the previous essay.

In the one-term (ten-week) courses we have taught, we like to see students in conference three times. The second of these, the midterm conference, allows us to review each student's progress and discuss the goals for the remainder of the course.

Individual Conferences

We find that the best length for individual conferences is half an hour, although it is possible to make some progress in twenty minutes if the time is spent carefully.

The student comes to the conference with a draft in hand and may at first expect you to play the role of mechanic, making the necessary repairs on it while he or she waits in anxious silence. It is often tempting to take the draft from the student and go to work on it, but this defeats the object of conferencing, which is to help students learn to work on their own drafts. To this end, we leave the draft in the student's hands for most of the conference and usually begin by asking the student to either read it aloud or talk about it. In the most successful conferences, the students do at least half the talking; our comments merely draw them out and let them make discoveries for themselves.

Students can come to conferences well prepared to talk about their drafts and to take responsibility for solving problems—if they have specific guidelines for preparing themselves. At the end of each of the individual Chapter Plans (Chapter 5 of this manual), we provide conference-planning forms for students to fill out, a form for each assignment in Part One of the text.

Small-Group Conferences

An alternative to the individual conference is the small-group conference. Instead of meeting with each student for half an hour, the instructor might meet with three students for an hour, spending twenty minutes on each student's draft. In a typical group conference, each student brings copies of his or her draft for the other two students and the instructor. They each read their drafts aloud while the listeners make notes on their copies. At the end of each reading, the instructor leads a discussion about the draft, with the other two students contributing their views and suggestions. After twenty minutes, the writer collects the annotated copies, and attention is turned to the next student's draft.

The group conference, which lacks the privacy of an individual conference, could intimidate shy students. However, the group may generate ideas that would not emerge in a one-on-one conference. Some of the comments we make about the first student's draft usually apply to the other two drafts as well, and students often decide to change their own drafts after the discussion of another student's draft. Neither conference format is inherently better than the other; we recommend that you try both to decide which you prefer.

Electronic Conferences

Instead of meeting face-to-face with individual students or in small groups, an instructor can hold conferences using a real-time messenger service or chat room. For commuting students, especially those with full-time jobs who have limited time on campus, these electronic modes of communication allow for an alternative means of getting immediate feedback on drafts, asking questions about assignments, or discussing other pressing matters.

ORGANIZING WORKSHOPS

The workshop brings class members together to read and respond to their work in progress—usually the first or second draft. There are many possible variations in the format of a workshop, including the following ones that have worked for us.

Written Response

Because students don't hear or remember everything a critical reader says about a draft, we find it helps when students write up their responses so that the writers can refer to them later when they actually revise. We also find that when students are given guidance and time, they can provide a very thoughtful, useful response—one that helps them as writers while also helping their workshop partner.

We typically begin by asking students to exchange their drafts with another class member. As students first exchange drafts, they brief their partners on particular points on which they would like feedback. Each student then spends ten to twenty minutes silently reading the partner's draft and writing a critical response to it. Activities and questions found in the Critical Reading Guide section in each of the chapters in Part One lead students through this process. They write their responses on separate sheets of paper, labeled at the top to look like this:

Proposal Essay Draft 2

Workshop Response for John Smith by Mary Jones

While students are working silently on each other's drafts, you may choose to move among them to offer advice. Alternatively, you could arrange in advance for one or two students to bring copies of their drafts for you to review during this time. When students have finished writing, they return the draft with their written comments, taking a few minutes to look over the response to their own essay and to ask their partner about anything confusing. To facilitate this critical exchange, you may want to pair students according to their writing abilities and change the pairs with each essay assignment so that each student receives comments from several others. Another option is to organize students into small groups instead of pairs, each group including some stronger and weaker writers.

Novice writers tend to write their first workshop responses with some anxiety. A few will launch into devastatingly honest evaluations of a partner's draft, but most err on the side of conciliation. Influenced perhaps by the knowledge that their own drafts are undergoing similar scrutiny, they are usually eager to praise and offer little substantial criticism. At the beginning of the course, they also lack the experience to make constructive recommendations to the writer.

One way to address this problem is to take students through the activities and questions in the Critical Reading Guide in the first workshop, modeling for them the kind of critique that would let the writer know what works, what needs help, and what might be done to revise the essay. A good response points to specific things in the draft, describes their effect on the reader honestly but tactfully, and suggests options the writer might consider. Questions to the writer beginning "How about . . . ?" are often useful. To model such a critique, you can use copies of a class member's draft, copies of an anonymous draft written for a similar assignment in a previous course, or a selection from *Sticks and Stones and other student essays.*

In computer-assisted composition courses, students can post their own drafts and respond to each other's on a class Web site. Students can also exchange drafts and critique them using email with essays and responses copied into the messages or sent as attachments.

Discussion

You can also organize the workshop around oral reading and response. One possibility is to arrange in advance for one or two students to bring enough copies of their drafts for the other class members to share — a copy for every two students. You can also use an overhead projector (having students first put their drafts on transparencies) or a computerized projection system, if one is available. The writer tells the class about any particular problems he or she has had with the draft and then reads it aloud while the rest of the class follows along on the copies, making marginal notes where appropriate. The class will respond better if they hear and see the draft simultaneously. At the end of the reading, the instructor chairs a discussion of the draft, appointing a scribe to record the comments for the writer. The activities and questions in the Critical Reading Guide can form the basis of this discussion. At the end of the discussion, the scribe gives the writer the discussion notes and other students pass along their copies with marginal notes.

This whole-class discussion of one draft at a time simulates the traditional writers' workshop widely used in MFA programs. Many instructors using this workshop format ask the writer not to participate in the discussion. There are good reasons for this rule. At the draft stage, writers need to know the immediate personal responses and evaluative reflections of readers. They need to listen to the discussion and reflect thoughtfully on what readers say, why they misunderstand, and what they have questions about. The writer needs to watch postures and facial expressions. Are the readers really interested in this draft, or is the discussion lifeless and perfunctory? What things do readers point to? What do they ignore? What seems to confuse them? What do they understand best and seem most pleased with? Is the discussion desultory, moving from one point to the next with little connection or sequence? Or does the discussion have a direction, with many people involved making their contributions? From watching this sort of discussion of one's draft, a writer can find out whether it struck readers as boring or engaging, pointless or informative, unsupported or convincing. The writer especially benefits if readers are specific and provide written reactions at the end of the workshop.

You may choose to begin a workshop with class discussion and then allow some time for students to exchange drafts and written analyses, so that you can review basic features and requirements of the assignment. Even with the Guide to Writing, there will still be students who have not yet brought the assignment into focus. By concentrating initially on one or two papers with the whole class, you can remind students of the basic features of that kind of writing. At the end of the discussion, you can summarize these basic features on the chalkboard and relate them to points in the Critical Reading Guide. This should give students more confidence in helping each other and keep them focused on the central issues of the assignment rather than the peripheral ones.

Working with the whole class on one draft also allows you to make observations that are relevant to the assignment and not just to the draft in hand. An alternative is to divide the class into small groups of four or five and to have one member of each group bring copies of his or her draft for the others in the group and read it aloud to them. If there is time, a group could respond to several students' drafts—at least superficially. In a large class, this allows more students to receive group responses to their drafts and encourages the more reticent students to participate in the discussion. You could join one group or move among the groups. This format works best when students know what is expected and can work productively without your guidance.

Practical Considerations

1. When a student comes to class late or without a draft, you have several options, depending on which workshop format the class is using:
   - Conduct a conference with the student.
   - Have the student join a pair and read a draft page by page as one partner finishes.
   - Have the student respond to a copy of a draft that has been duplicated for the whole class.

In all these cases, the student must be reminded that he or she is responsible for obtaining another student's response to his or her own draft. You could require the student to get a written comment from a writing center tutor. Specify that the tutor should follow the guidelines for the Critical Reading Guide.

2. You can choose whether to have students work in pairs or small groups or whether to lead a discussion in which the entire class participates.

3. When the first and second drafts of the same assignment are read in subsequent workshops, some instructors ask students to choose a different partner to respond to the second draft. Other instructors allow students to choose the same partner to read the second draft, so that the partner can comment on the progress the writer has made since the first draft.

4. Some instructors find it useful to have students put their phone numbers or email addresses on their workshop responses, so that writers can contact their workshop partners if they find they have questions as they revise their drafts.

5. Some instructors ask all students to bring an extra copy of their drafts. During the workshop, while pairs are quietly writing their critiques of each other's drafts, the instructor quickly reviews all drafts, noting the most glaring problems.

ASSIGNING JOURNALS

Many writing teachers appreciate the value of journals in a writing course. The brevity, frequency, and informality of entries in a journal allow students to use writing in many more ways than they do in formal essays. In our courses, students keep a journal in which they respond to Connecting to Culture and Experience and Analyzing Writing Strategies following every Part One reading in the *Concise Guide,* to Part Two exercises, or to further questions and assignments provided by their instructors. Journal assignments can be used to challenge students to engage in a wide range of critical thinking activities, including responding to readings and practicing various thinking and writing strategies. Although journal entries are most often written outside of class, they can also be written in class—for example, to begin discussion of the reading, to summarize a discussion, or to reflect on what they have learned, perhaps by using the metacognitive activity at the end of each Part One chapter.

Practical Considerations: Assigning, Monitoring, and Responding to Journal Questions

Some instructors hand out a weekly set of three to five journal tasks, which may include tasks and activities from the *Concise Guide,* while others provide students at the beginning of the term with a list of tasks for the entire course, specifying weekly due dates. A few instructors collect journal entries only every few weeks; most, however, find it worthwhile collecting and re-sponding to them on a weekly basis. Although some instructors ask students to keep their journals in spiral-bound notebooks, you may want to have your students write each journal entry on a separate sheet of looseleaf note-book paper, labeled with their name, the week number, and the number of the entry (or whatever information best facilitates your record-keeping sys-tem). This makes collecting students' completed journal entries for each week somewhat easier and enables them to use a computer if they like.

Students could also submit one entry a week to a class listserv or elec-tronic bulletin board to share with other members of the class. You might then ask them each to choose one other student's journal entry, write a re-sponse to it, and send the response to the list. Journal entries would then contribute to a shared body of knowledge, and students would get feedback from their classmates as well as from you. Responding to journal entries need not be time-consuming. A few suggestions or words of encouragement in the margins are generally sufficient to let students see that you've read their entries. Although some instructors use informal marking systems such as plusses, checks, and minuses, journal entries really should not be graded or judged for mechanical correctness. Instead, they should be evaluated for quantity and quality of thought. It is important that students understand from the very beginning that the journal, although informal, is neither a pri-vate diary nor busy-work but a serious component of the course, and that you expect their journal entries to be thorough, thoughtful, and even provocative.

Planning a Sequence of Journal Questions

It takes careful planning to coordinate your own journal assignments with the reading selections for the course. A planned sequence of journal ques-tions allows students to reflect on what they have learned and to see connec-tions among the various components of your course. In particular, journal questions can help them make connections between the assigned readings and their own writing.

Sample Journal Questions

In general, journal assignments help students improve their writing skills by exercising their critical reading and thinking skills. Journal questions can guide students to identify certain strategies in the texts they're reading and then practice these strategies in their own writing. The following list of kinds of questions, which is by no means exhaustive, suggests a range of possibilities for journal assignments.

Analyzing and Responding to Readings.   Some instructors use the journal exclusively for this purpose, calling it a Reader's Journal instead of a Writer's Journal. They ask their students to answer questions following the readings in Part One chapters, as well as questions they pose about trade books they have assigned. Consider also assigning critical reading strategies from Chapter 10 or inviting students to select the ones they find most useful.

See the discussion in the next section, Presenting and Discussing Readings, for ideas about using journal writing to encourage critical reading and to prepare for class discussions of assigned readings.

Applying Rhetorical Strategies. Other questions help students apply strategies they see in their reading to their own essays:

> In Chapter 8: Strategies for Cueing Readers, you learned about various strategies to make your writing more readable. Discuss one cueing strategy that would remedy a particular weakness that you have or that someone else has noticed in your writing. Give an example of the problem in your writing, showing how you would use this cueing device to solve it.

Experimenting and Adapting. Many questions of this type encourage students to experiment with general rhetorical strategies and to adapt these strategies to different types of discourse. These questions, some of which refer to reading passages provided by the instructor, help students develop an awareness of the many choices involved in taking a particular rhetorical stance, among them voice, style, and tone.

> Take an issue that you know a lot about and argue for or against it in the most *unauthoritative* voice you can.
>
> "Translate" some fine writing into bureaucratese, as George Orwell did with the following biblical passage. Then reflect on what makes the writing good in one passage and bad in the other.
>
>> I returned and saw under the sun, that the race is not to the swift, nor the battle to the strong, neither yet bread to the wise, nor yet riches to men of understanding, nor yet favor to men of skill; but time and chance happen to them all.
>>
>> Objective consideration of contemporary phenomena compels the conclusion that success or failure in competitive activities exhibits no tendency to be commensurate with innate capacity, but that a considerable element of the unpredictable must invariably be taken into account.

Preparing to Write Formal Essays. Some journal assignments help students prepare to write their own essays by testing ideas, practicing parts of essays, or writing mini-essays that develop one basic feature of the genre. This type of journal question can be used as a supplement to the invention sequence for each Part One assignment:

> Write a mini-evaluation of one of your former teachers, developing one reason for your evaluation. One full page should be adequate. Be sure

to follow the guidelines discussed in class and outlined in Chapter 7: Justifying an Evaluation.

Write two different thesis paragraphs for the essay proposing a solution. You may want to try casting the same idea in two different ways, or you may offer very different problems and solutions in each. State both of these and indicate how you are going to support each one.

Practicing Editing Skills.   Some journal questions may ask students to practice editing skills ranging from punctuation to the use and acknowledgment of sources.

Make a works cited list for books used in this class, a short story in an anthology, a magazine article, a newspaper article, and a Web site.

Photocopy a page from your evaluation essay and staple it to your journal entry. Then do some close editing as we did in class today.

Reflecting on Your Learning.   Finally, you could use the journal as a place for students to reflect on what they are learning in your course as well as in other courses. The metacognitive activity at the end of each Part One chapter could be used here, or you could devise additional journal questions.

How would you describe yourself as a writer at the beginning of the term? In what ways have you changed as a writer over the term?

Looking back over your other courses this term, list the kinds of writing you had to do. Then choose one kind of writing and describe its basic features.

You will no doubt think of still other ways of using a journal to complement the *Concise Guide*.

PRESENTING AND DISCUSSING READINGS

Reading plays a very important role in a writing course. We encourage students to read as writers—to examine not only the content of a text but also various features and strategies they can adapt for use in their own writing. We also want them to learn to read with a critical eye—to question rather than accept unsupported assertions, to differentiate between fact and opinion, to evaluate arguments, and to examine assumptions. Chapter 10 presents an array of critical reading strategies, and each Part One chapter follows readings with questions on Connecting to Culture and Experience and Analyzing Writing Strategies. These could be used as the basis for small-group or whole-class discussion. We emphasize that our courses are discussion seminars and that we expect every student to participate in the discussions.

Helping Students Prepare for Successful Discussions

For discussions of the readings to succeed, we try to ensure not only that students have done the reading carefully, but also that they are prepared to discuss it—with us and with each other. Instructors can use many different strategies both for ensuring that students do the reading in the first place and for guiding them to get the most out of class discussions.

Encouraging Students to Do the Reading.   Simply letting students know in the syllabus that they will be expected to answer journal questions and participate in discussions (and that they will be evaluated on their journals and class participation) is enough to motivate most students, most of the time. However, many instructors find it worthwhile to take further measures to ensure that all of the students do all of the reading.

Nearly all instructors assign journal questions on the readings as homework and then call on several students at random to read their journal entries aloud at the beginning of class. Some instructors use in-class journal questions on the readings as quizzes. Since the topics of these questions are not announced in advance, students know that they must complete the assigned reading to be prepared. You could use an informal grading system to arrive at a "preparation grade" for the course.

Helping Students Get the Most out of the Reading.   Experienced writing teachers know that asking the right questions can encourage close reading. Carefully planned journal questions—questions that do not merely test students' comprehension but ask students to read critically and to examine the text's rhetorical features and strategies—help students read carefully and allow them to make thoughtful contributions to classroom discussion. The discussion and analysis questions which follow each reading in Part One of the *Concise Guide* are questions of this type.

Although annotation is not required in our assignments, students find it an indispensable technique for critical reading. Annotating is particularly useful in preparing students for discussions of the readings, as their annotations serve to remind them in the classroom of the features and patterns they note as they read each piece. Annotating is illustrated in Chapter 10: Strategies for Reading Critically. Many instructors ask students to read some texts not once but several times, annotating for different features each time. They prepare students to annotate by listing and discussing these features. For instance, students might annotate first for structure and organization, then for the basic features of the genre, and finally to note the writer's particular rhetorical strategies.

Because the idea of annotation is likely to be new to most students, many instructors find it helpful to prepare students for making their own annotations by providing a sample of a thoroughly annotated text or by talking students through a page of text as they annotate it. It is also a good idea to collect students' earliest tries at annotation to monitor and encourage their attempts. Chapter 10 offers many other critical reading strategies you can use as the basis for class discussion, such as looking for opposition, reflecting on challenges to your beliefs, and evaluating reasoning or credibility.

Facilitating Successful Classroom Discussions

Remind students of the connection between the readings and their own writing. To begin, you could call on several students to read their answers to journal questions, or you could pair students up to work on different parts of a reading and then have them report their findings to the class. The aim is to involve them from the start in an active examination of the text and also to engage them in a collaborative effort of some kind. We find the best way to do this is to ask "real" questions that require close analysis, for example, of how a particular strategy works or falls short. (Here you can rely on the Analyzing Writing Strategies section following each reading.)

To complete the discussion, ask students to summarize the main things they have learned. Some instructors go around the room, asking students to indicate a strategy they could imagine trying in their own writing or, conversely, something they would try to avoid doing. They might also compare and contrast different readings in a chapter. A principal aim of discussing reading in a writing course, we think, is to show students that they can write as effectively as—or even more effectively than—the professional and student writers whose work they're reading.

Some Practical Considerations

Give up on discussions that don't seem to be going anywhere or that aren't engaging most of the students. Do not stay on a single point (or a single essay) for too long. Instead, keep up the pace so that students stay attentive.

Try to involve every student in every discussion so that a few students are not doing all the talking. Some students are shy about speaking in class, and involving them may take extra effort on your part. One way to elicit a spoken response from even the shyest of students is to ask a simple, low-key question such as, "What is memorable about the piece?" Most students should be able to answer this question on the spot, and they can be encouraged to elaborate on their answers.

Group activities are a good way of getting students involved in discussions. Some instructors assign each essay in a chapter to a group of three or four students and ask each group to annotate the essay, either for a set of features or for a single feature. Each group then leads the discussion of its essay, beginning by reporting its observations to the rest of the class. This type of activity is particularly useful for involving students in discussion; the students in the audience are aware that they too will have to lead the class discussion, and this awareness makes them more likely to contribute.

In networked computer classrooms or for online courses, students can hold synchronous or real-time discussions using chat rooms, Multi-User Domains (MUDs), and MUDs Object-Oriented (MOOs). Students engage in a written discussion, which can be printed and used as the basis for future discussion or writing. As with other forms of discussion, you can play an active role or intervene only when necessary.

SETTING UP COLLABORATIVE LEARNING GROUPS

Collaborative learning has always been central, of course, to writing-workshop courses and to any composition course in which students discuss work in progress. For quite a while now, experienced, informed writing instructors have seen themselves as collaborators in improving students' composing, rather than as error sleuths or test givers or even as evaluators. And there is growing interest in collaborative writing within composition studies, as there are many occasions in academia, business, and other professions when two or more writers need to collaborate to produce a single piece of writing. Several of the writing assignments in Part One lend themselves very well to collaboration. Explaining concepts (Chapter 4), especially if based on research, works well, but writing profiles (Chapter 3) seems to require such a strong vision to put together all the information and impressions, that it is harder to bring off effectively. Any of the argument chapters—5 through 7—could be used. Collaborating on the position paper would be especially challenging if students' views on the issue were opposed. The proposal is the most obvious choice, and the one most often written collaboratively outside the classroom.

Collaborative Learning Assignments

If time permits, you could ask students to meet in small groups outside of class to discuss readings and either plan an oral report or complete specific tasks. These meetings could be occasions primarily for rereading and talking, though some writing might result as well.

Here are two basic activities you might try if you wish to set up collaborative reading groups.

Group Report on a Reading

Carefully read the essay assigned to your group and then meet with the other members to prepare a presentation for the class. You may be asked to respond to the Connecting to Culture and Experience or Analyzing Writing Strategies tasks following the reading, or to a question posed in class.

You should expect other members of the class to be familiar with the essay you will present. Needless to say, you should be familiar with the essays assigned to the other groups and prepared to participate in the discussions about these essays.

Group Evaluation of Two Readings

Your group has been assigned two readings. Carefully read the two essays before you meet with your group. Before you read, though, review the Basic Features section. Then, as you read both readings, take notes on how they fulfill the basic features of the genre. Decide on your own which reading you think is more effective and why.

Then meet with your group and discuss each person's choice. Try to arrive at a consensus. If you cannot agree, feel free to file minority and majority reports. In your report (or reports), you should explain your group's judgment and the reasons for making it.

You should expect other members of the class to be familiar with these essays. Needless to say, you should be familiar with the essays assigned to the other groups and prepared to participate in the other groups' presentations of their evaluations.

There are many possible variations on these basic activities. For example, for the evaluate-two-readings activity, you could ask groups to report on similarities and differences between the two readings rather than to argue that one is more effective than the other.

How do you arrange collaborative reading groups? As soon as possible, assign each student to a group of four. You may have one group of three or five, but five have greater difficulty in finding a common meeting time than four, and three are sometimes reduced to two and then are not really a group. If students drop out during the term, you may need to combine reduced groups. Try to avoid homogeneous groupings. We recommend a mix of different genders, cultural backgrounds, ages, or other factors to ensure a heterogeneous group. You may also want to ensure a range of abilities in each group. After you've formed the groups, give them an opportunity to meet in class so that they can schedule a regular meeting time outside of class or to exchange email addresses so that they can communicate electronically.

Explain to them that the collaborative discussion of readings will contribute to their success in your course and offer them general guidelines for collaboration. Their goal—at least in these two basic activities—is to prepare a brief report (five to eight minutes, depending on how many groups you have and how long your class meets) on what they learn about the readings. Tell them they must report as a panel, with each person contributing. Since the reports tend to sprawl, you will have to enforce time limits so that all groups may report and you will have time for other activities.

CONDUCTING COMMUNITY SERVICE LEARNING PROJECTS

Another area gaining increasing interest and scholarly attention is community service learning, in which students participate in activities outside the classroom, within a particular community, and write with a specific public audience in mind. Involving students in community service while they are enrolled in a composition course enables them to take part in projects that increase their civic awareness and prepare them for future roles as engaged citizens. In addition, they gain an understanding of writing as a social act and an increased recognition of the importance of the rhetorical dimensions of specific kinds of writing.

Several of the writing assignments in Part One of the *Concise Guide* reflect the kind of writing that might actually occur outside of the classroom. These assignments are also well suited to community service, which involves students in working through real issues that affect their communities. The following assignments could include a community service learning component:

- Writing Profiles
- Arguing a Position
- Proposing a Solution
- Justifying an Evaluation

Students can interview elderly people involved in neighborhood programs and write profiles of them, which can be published in an anthology or on a Web page. They can also submit editorials to the op-ed page of the local newspaper or send proposals in the form of letters to local officials or government bodies. These assignments can be completed by individual students or in collaboration with other students. Students can also collaborate with individuals outside the academic setting—members of specific community groups or organizations, for example.

You might allow students to choose their own projects in their own neighborhoods, or you might set up projects with non-profit organizations. The latter may require extensive preparation on your part, unless your institution already has a community service program. In general, though, you will find staff people in these organizations eager to work with educational institutions and ready with project ideas. To make community service learning projects work, you should be sensitive to the kinds of problems students may face. Some may have difficulty getting to a project site far from campus. Asking students to share transportation or limiting projects to the campus community might solve this problem. Students may also have difficulties making connections with staff people in the organizations or measuring up to expectations of professional behavior. It might be necessary to remind them that they are representing not just themselves but also the university or college in a public forum. You might need to discuss codes of conduct as obvious as keeping appointments or arriving on time.

For additional sources on conducting community service learning projects, see the bibliography in the appendix of this manual.

Evaluation Practices

2

This chapter includes some general advice about responding to student writing, assigning portfolios, and responding to error.

GENERAL GUIDELINES FOR RESPONDING TO STUDENT WRITING

This section offers general suggestions for responding to invention work, drafts, and revisions. It opens with a discussion of the basis for response, pointing to the sources of criteria and standards within each of the writing assignment chapters (2–7) in the *Concise Guide*.

The Criteria for Response

We need to consider first the basis for response, which comes from the writer's purpose and intended audience and from the genre constraints and possibilities of the particular writing situation. Some possible purposes and stances toward readers are addressed in the Purpose and Audience discussion of each of the writing assignment chapters (2–7). The characteristic though varied patterning of discourse features and writing strategies that define each genre are discussed and illustrated in the commentaries following the readings and the Basic Features section.

These basic features and strategies become criteria for responding to a draft or revision when, with the student's purpose and readers in mind, you (or other students) ask: Given his or her purpose and readers, has the writer finally realized the possibilities of this genre? How well has the writer used the features and strategies he or she has chosen to achieve the purpose with the intended reader? These general questions are treated in several places in each writing assignment chapter:

- Analyzing Writing Strategies questions following each reading
- Testing Your Choice: A Collaborative Activity in the Invention section
- Setting Goals in the Planning and Drafting section

- Critical Reading Guide
- Carrying Out Revisions in the Revising section

They are illustrated, discussed, or experienced directly in various other places in Chapters 2–7, including the writing scenarios, the collaborative activities, and the readings and their commentaries.

Axelrod & Cooper's Concise Guide to Writing makes explicit its expectations of students. By the time they've worked their way through a chapter — analyzing readings, studying commentaries, reviewing basic features, completing invention — they should, if they've been at all alert, be ready to draft an essay which reflects a good understanding of the genre. With the help of the Critical Reading Guide, they should then be prepared to respond confidently to a draft and to comprehend any suggestions that you or other readers might offer. When they revise, the suggestions for Carrying Out Revisions should seem almost predictable. They should, in other words, know the criteria for evaluating writing of the type they are attempting. And having come this far with them, you should be confident about evaluating their final drafts.

Principles of Response

With this basis for response as a starting point, what principles might guide an instructor's response to student writing? From long experience in the classroom and from devotion to the growing literature in composition studies, we've settled on the following principles:

- Students need response to their work at every stage of composition, not just at the revision stage. Response to a topic choice, to initial invention work, or to a first draft may be decisive in enabling the student to produce a revised essay that invites and justifies your thoughtful evaluation.

- Response at the draft stage should support revision and encourage a student to persist through one or more revisions.

- Response to errors in grammar, usage, punctuation, and spelling should be reserved for later drafts.

- In order for response to lead to motivated, productive revision, it must take the student's purpose and audience, the particular ideas in the essay, and the constraints and possibilities of the genre into account. General advice, interchangeable from one essay to the next, is usually less helpful than genre-specific response.

- Students most of all need their teachers to be genuine readers of their work, not merely judges and error hunters. A readerly response helps students understand that writing is an important and irreplaceable form of interaction with others. It also helps them to imagine readers' responses as they write.

- Response to drafts and revisions should be selective. Novice writers, like beginners at any complex human performance, can be overwhelmed and discouraged by too much advice.

- Students in a writing course should form a collaborative-learning community. They should read and respond to one another's writing, and help each other solve problems in their writing.

Responding at the Invention Stage

If you require students to complete all of the invention work—as we do in our programs—you may want to devote some class time to invention, for coaching and response. We usually complete the first two steps in class, first listing topics and then choosing one. A whole-class effort always produces many more promising topics than students can come up with on their own. Students list some topics alone, and then we make one big list on the board including everyone's topics. Some instructors begin evaluating topics at this stage, pointing out both those that are problematic and those that are promising, and encouraging students to comment on what they would expect from essays on the proposed topics. Helping students see the implications of topic choice engages them in the process from the start.

You may also wish to schedule time for students to start exploring their topics in class. We ask three or four students to read these invention notes aloud and then comment on what they are learning. Our purpose is to overcome the strangeness of systematic invention work—few students, if any, have ever done it—and to help students see what productive invention writing might look like.

Many instructors find it best to set due dates over the next week or so for the remaining stages of invention work. We may again ask a few students to read certain parts aloud or allow some class time for them to work in small groups, to talk to each other about what they are learning about their topics through their invention work. This can also be a good time for students to be analyzing chapter readings or, if you have already discussed the readings, you might want to review specific aspects of those readings or essays in *Sticks and Stones,* the collection of student essays that accompanies the *Concise Guide.* Because the essays in *Sticks and Stones* were all written for the writing assignments in the *Concise Guide,* they serve as trustworthy examples of the kind of writing students using our text are working to produce.

When the invention work has been completed, it helps to have brief conferences with students to find out whether they are getting something from the invention activities. Skimming a student's invention writing, you cannot predict how the final essay will turn out, but we know from many years of coaching and observation that the most productive invention work has an exploratory, even playful, quality. It is specific, or concrete, rather than general. It follows up on images, pushing ideas rather than letting them drop. It is sometimes digressive and fragmentary, and it is relatively lengthy. It is rarely brief or cautious, and never perfunctory. We try to comment briefly on students' work in these terms, and, with students' permission, we may photocopy four or five promising examples of invention work to show the class.

Responding at the Draft Stage

Responses at the draft stage can come in peer workshops (meeting in class or out), conferences with you, or from you in writing.

In Workshops. The key workshop resource in the *Concise Guide* is the Critical Reading Guide section in each of the writing assignment chapters (2–7). These guidelines begin by helping students prepare their drafts for a critical reader by stating their purposes and describing their readers. Then, after exchanging drafts, they can use all or some of the questions to analyze a draft and advise the writer about possible revisions. We usually ask students to write out their analyses in order to provide the writer with a record of suggestions for revision. Peer discussion tends to be especially productive after students have done this kind of thoughtful written analysis. We generally follow written response with discussion, which can then be quite specific and substantive.

We find that we need to prepare students to respond to one another's work. To do so, we might distribute one or two student essays to the class or project essays on a screen and walk students through the questions in the Critical Reading Guide, modeling specific, constructive responses.

There are countless variations on this workshop scheme, all of them with merit. Advantages we claim for our scheme are that students follow assignment-specific guidelines and write before they talk. We usually join in group discussions, instead of just looking on or listening in.

In Conferences. The key to successful conferences is getting students to prepare carefully so that when they come to see you, they can do most of the talking and take much of the responsibility for improving their drafts.

To help students prepare, we developed a form to fill in before coming to the conference, a different form for each writing assignment. You will find these specially designed forms for each of the writing assignments in the *Concise Guide,* ready for you to reproduce, in Chapter 5 of this manual. In conference, we usually begin with one of these forms. But we may also draw students' attention to one or two especially relevant parts of the Critical Reading Guide so that they see that we are applying the criteria consistently.

Responding at the Revision Stage

By the time students complete an essay assignment, they will have generated a good deal of writing. For instructors, the goal is to have a system of reading and responding to it that allows them to give students helpful feedback and still process the pile of student work in a reasonable amount of time.

Helping Students Organize an Assignment Package. You need to tell students exactly what materials are to be turned in with the final, revised essay. At the beginning of the course, we give students a handout that specifies what they are to turn in for each writing assignment. We ask for the following materials:

1. Revision: The final, revised version of the essay, typed and proofread, with any errors neatly corrected. It should be double-spaced, typed on one side of the page only, and numbered.

2. Reflecting on Your Writing: Students analyze their problem-solving processes in writing and revising the paper.

3. A List of Problems in the Draft: From the analysis completed in the Revising section of the *Concise Guide*.

4. Critical Comments: Written comments about one draft, done by a classmate. The classmate's name should be on the response.

5. Drafts: One or more drafts, legible and labeled with the student's name, the assignment title, and the draft number. The pages should be numbered.

6. Invention and Planning Notes

We also ask students to put this work together with a large paper clip rather than in a bulky file folder. We find this assignment package reduces confusion, eases our management of the large amounts of writing, and speeds the reading and response process.

Before reading the package, you might read the student's written reflections in response to Reflecting on Your Writing. This activity, with its focus on how the student identified and solved a problem in the essay, presents a self-portrait of the student as a writer. We try to applaud the student's problem-solving efforts to bolster the student's confidence and encourage revising. We might draw the student's attention to another problem that needs solving and invite another revision focusing on this problem.

Surveying the Package and Completing Records.   We start by skimming to see that all the assigned writing is there and to see what the student has accomplished in the invention and drafts. The invention tends to be a good indicator of the depth and thoroughness of the revised essay, and problems in the revision can often be traced to deficiencies in invention. We try to make this connection clear to students early in the course. We keep track of each student's performance at all the various stages of the composing process for each assignment on a record sheet that you will find later in this chapter, ready for you to reproduce. This sheet is for our own records, and students do not see it.

The students' self-evaluation (Reflecting on Your Writing in Chapters 2–7) prompts them to reflect critically on their composing process, to think about what they have written, and to take responsibility for the decisions they have made. At its worst, such a self-evaluation will say no more than "here-it-is-I-like-it-hope-you-do-too," as the student declines the invitation to take responsibility. At its best, however, the student creates an account of his or her composing process, which provides you with a critical introduction to the essay. The self-evaluation can also reveal the student's level of involvement with the assignment. We usually read the self-evaluation carefully.

Responding to the Revised Essay.   Plan to spend several minutes responding to the revision. We make a few comments in the margins, noting both strong and weak points in the writing, and then we add a few sentences of comments at the end, on a separate sheet of paper. You may want to keep a copy of these comments for your own records. We try to find something in the essay to praise, and we find that critical comments work best when phrased in terms of what the student might have done in the essay or should try to do in the next one. Questions are useful, too, when they lead students to think about other ways they might have addressed the problems in the paper. This approach casts the instructor in the role of reader/adviser rather than of judge.

You can use all or part of the Critical Reading Guide to focus on particular features in the essay in order of priority. In an autobiographical essay, for example, we begin by considering the larger rhetorical issues: the significance, the narrative structure, and the vividness of descriptive details. Next, we look at some particular features of the genre: the use of dialogue and the proportion of narration, description, and commentary in the story. (In Chapter 5, you will find brief guidelines for responding to each of the assignments in the *Concise Guide,* listing the criteria for response and some typical problems.) Finally, we comment on grammar, usage, punctuation, and style.

We advise against commenting on everything that could be improved in a paper. An inexperienced writer can be easily overwhelmed by too much criticism and become too discouraged to work on any of the problems. Rather, we try to focus on a few of the most important issues that need attention, thereby giving the student achievable goals. We follow the same policy with grammatical errors and stylistic infelicities, assuming that if we mark every transgression in a weak writer's paper, the student may be overwhelmed. Later in this chapter is a plan for dealing with students' errors.

Finally, if time allows, we encourage (and may even require) a student to revise again. A series of revisions focusing on one problem at a time can lead to significant improvement in the essay and a better understanding of how to use the process to write an essay students can be proud of.

Some General Guidelines for Responding to Revised Essays

1. Check the package to be sure that all of the required parts are there. Note missing parts and comment on parts (the invention, for example) that please or disappoint you.

2. Read the revision through quickly to get the sense of it. Is it what you assigned? Does it look approximately right?

3. Decide first whether the package needs to be returned for further work before you can evaluate it. There are several reasons why you might want the student to do some additional work before you evaluate the package:

   - The package is substantially incomplete: The invention, workshop responses, self-evaluation, or one or more drafts are missing, or perhaps only the final revision is there.
   - The final revision is not typed, or is otherwise unreadable because of printer problems, worn-out ribbons, etc.
   - The revision does not meet the genre requirements of the rhetorical situation: It is a problem solution essay rather than a position paper, an event essay rather than a concept explanation, an evaluation essay without adequate evidence from the thing being evaluated, and so on.
   - The topic does not fall within the constraints of your assignment. (For example, you might have declared dormitory problems off-limits for the problem solution essay, and yet the student wrote about a dormitory problem.)
   - The revision is seriously disorganized.
   - The revision has major problems with grammar, punctuation, or usage.

   If you return an essay package for further work, outline your reasons briefly, and ask the student to make an appointment for a conference to discuss his or her plan for revising. You might ask the student to review the readings and the Basic Features for this essay in the *Concise Guide*. Set a deadline (from one to two weeks) for resubmitting the package. You want to make it clear that although the package does not yet meet your standards, you are convinced that the student is capable of succeeding with this writing assignment. You might ask the writer to (a) start over with a new topic, (b) substantially revise an entire draft, or (c) revise only one part of a draft.

4. If the revision is ready to be evaluated, look first for the strengths in the paper. What did the student do well or at least satisfactorily? Try to comment on some aspects of the paper of which you approve.

5. Does the revision show a grasp of the specific features of its type of writing? Usually, some features are represented more successfully than others. Which ones are handled well? Which ones could have been developed more successfully?

6. Does the revision seem coherent and organized? Are the transitions from one part to the next handled smoothly? Comment on structural elements that work well or that might be improved.

7. What about errors? We expect revised essays to have been carefully edited and proofread, but most students are just learning to edit their own writing. Since even the best essays often have some sentence-level problems, we usually identify substantive issues and then return the

paper to the student for another round of editing. We also find it help-ful for students to keep a record of their common errors to guide proof-reading and editing. This procedure reinforces the importance of editing, but puts it in its proper place — at the end of the writing process.

Grading.   Some instructors do not grade individual essays, though you may wish to. One argument against grading individual essays is that a letter grade is at best a cryptic indication of performance, and that grades on individual essays can involve instructor and students in unproductive appeals and justi-fications. Furthermore, the risk of a low grade can discourage an inexperi-enced writer from taking creative chances.

Of course, students need some indication of their progress before the obligatory letter grades at the end of the course, so some instructors fill out midterm progress reports for all students, indicating what grades they can expect at the end of the course if they continue at their present levels of per-formance. This form shows students where they need to focus their atten-tion in the remainder of the course.

At the end of the course, these instructors use a final course report form to write a response to the final essay submitted and an evaluative summary of the student's performance in the whole course. (You will find these forms, ready to reproduce, later in this chapter.) This summary, and the course grade, are based on a quick review of a student's revised essays turned in along with the revision of the final essay. Also, considered are records of a student's attendance, reading journal entries, quizzes, workshop responses, and any other assigned work. The final grade is based on three criteria:

1. Whether all the assigned work has been completed in a timely fashion
2. Whether the work has improved during the course
3. Whether revised essays are fully realized rhetorically; that is, whether the student's revisions reveal substantial learning about the rhetorical and composing possibilities of the various genres assigned in the course

A Computer-Based Scheme for Responding to Student Writing

The widespread use of computers has had a significant effect on writing in-struction. Many students type journal responses and final drafts of their es-says on computers, and increasing numbers of students use computers for all stages of their composing process. In some classes, students submit their es-says on disks or electronically into a computer folder. Instructors use com-puters for a wide variety of teaching applications, from keeping student records to preparing daily lesson plans.

There are many useful commercial software programs available, includ-ing spreadsheet programs, database programs, and even specialized educational record-keeping packages. Unless you have several hundred students or the need for sophisticated statistical breakdowns or test-score reports, however, a basic word-processing program is all you need to keep track of student progress in a course using *Axelrod & Cooper's Concise Guide to Writing.*

One program, Microsoft Word, has a text-formatting feature called "hidden text." This text appears on the screen, but it does not print unless you use a special "print hidden text" command. This feature can be used to screen out your personal notes from your response to the student essay. You simply format any personal notes as hidden text. These notes can then be viewed on the screen or printed out for filing. The same document can be printed out for the student, with your personal notes hidden.

Your personal notes can be used for a wide range of purposes. Here you can comment, for example, on the student's need for campus support services, or on his or her class participation or helpfulness in collaborative groups. Later, you can work these observations about the student into responses to essays or into the midterm or final evaluation: "Your usage and style are much improved in this essay. Your sessions with the peer tutors seem to have paid off." "I notice you are always prepared for this class. This should give you confidence in contributing more often to class discussions."

If your word-processing program does not have a "hidden text" feature, you can easily create two files, pasting text from one file into the other. One file would contain your response to a student's essay, and the other file would contain both your response and your private comments under "Notes to the Instructor."

When you print out the response for the student, at the same time you can print out another copy with the hidden text printed to put into the student file for later evaluation at midterm and at the end of the course. Then, when it is time to evaluate the student, you will have an up-to-date file with one set of comments for each assignment. Having this hard copy is also good security against data loss in case you experience problems with your computer or the disk.

RESPONDING TO ERROR

Responding to students' errors in grammar, mechanics, usage, and punctuation is no small matter in a writing course. First, it is not easy to reduce students' errors; second, it is all too easy for efforts at reducing errors to dominate a writing course, crowding out time for reading, thinking, and composing. Following are some widely accepted principles for dealing with error in a first-year college writing course:

- Attention to error must not prevent students from spending most of their time reading, discussing, inventing, researching, planning, drafting, and revising extended, multiparagraph discourse. This principle holds for all students, no matter how high their initial error rate.

- Too much emphasis on error limits students' focus to local sentence problems, when they should be focusing on what they want to say and how they can best communicate to their particular readers. Overattention to error makes students cautious when they need to be taking chances, both to discover something to say and to find the sentences with which to say it.

- Standard edited English is best acquired through intensive reading, writing, and revising than learned through grammar study, rules and maxims, and exercises.

- If grammatical concepts are taught directly, they should be taught thoroughly by providing students background information, adequate definitions, diverse examples carefully discussed, and practice with feedback. Too often, textbook explanations of grammatical concepts are clear to students only if they already know the concepts.

- Error should become the focus of attention when students are editing and proofreading final drafts.

- The goal of instruction should be to help students take responsibility for finding, diagnosing, and correcting their own errors.

- If students, with the help of their instructors, analyze their errors, they will find patterns of common errors in their own writing . Identifying these patterns can help students simplify their efforts at overcoming those errors.

- Instruction in error-correction must be individualized. Whole-class instruction in grammar, usage, or style should occur only occasionally, if at all.

- Students need to learn how to use a handbook effectively to identify and correct errors.

These principles can guide your dealings with error even for students whose error rate is high, who speak a nonstandard dialect, or who still struggle with English as a second language. Following are two interrelated strategies we use to help our students learn to avoid error or edit their own writing. First, we teach them to identify and correct their own errors by marking the errors we find in a portion of their revised essays. As you can see in the handout on the following page, we underline the error and either put a check or the error code from the students' handbook in the margin. We focus on one section of the essay, such as a paragraph or a page, and try to identify every error we find in that section. The key to this approach is the follow-up, which requires students to use the handbook to decide how to correct the marked sentence. Students rewrite these sentences and we review their work, asking them to try again if they have not corrected the error satisfactorily.

Our second strategy follows from the first. We ask students to keep a chart of their common errors, including the handbook code and name of the error, one or more examples of their own sentences with the error and their corrections, and any other notes that will help them remember how to identify and correct the error. Students should use this chart when they proofread and edit their revised essays. In conference, we review the chart with students and help them analyze their common patterns of error. We may devote class time to discussing certain error patterns shared by many students in the class. We also sometimes use the error charts to construct groups for an editing workshop on the day students hand in their revised essays.

CORRECTING SENTENCE-LEVEL ERRORS IN REVISIONS

When I read your revised essay, I will first read for your ideas, logic, and use of sources, and I will evaluate in writing what you have accomplished. Then, I will mark off a section of your essay—a paragraph, a page, sometimes more—and analyze it closely for sentence-level errors. Like a newspaper or book editor, I will look for all the places where you have not observed the conventions of standard edited English.

I will indicate any line in which there is a sentence-level error by putting a check in the margin. Two checks indicate two errors. I will also underline the error itself, and I may code one or more errors so that you can find information about them in your handbook. The code will lead you to the page that will give you information about how to correct the error you have made.

After you have corrected all of your errors, I will check them. Here is what you do:

1. Number each error.
2. With the help of the handbook, identify each error and decide how to correct it.
3. On a separate piece of paper, rewrite every sentence in which there is an error. Do not write out just part of the sentence. *Write out the entire sentence,* unless you are correcting a misspelling.
4. Number your new sentences so that they correspond to the numbered errors.

If you cannot identify an error or figure out how to correct it, catch me after class or come to see me during my office hours.

This approach to error provides a highly efficient way for you to reduce errors in your writing. It is efficient for you and for me: I mark every error in just a small part of your writing instead of unsystematically marking an occasional error in all of your writing, and you work only on your own errors and learn quickly how to use a writer's handbook. Also, we do not waste time going over errors some of your classmates made but you did not make. You come to recognize the kinds of errors you make and learn ways to correct them. Most important, by correcting your own errors you learn how to avoid them. As a college student, you must learn as quickly as possible how to observe the conventions of standard edited English. When you are inventing and drafting, you need not be overly concerned with conventions. However, when you have revised an essay and are ready to present it as your best work, you must attend carefully to conventions.

MIDTERM PROGRESS REPORT

Student _____   Course _____

Instructor _____   Section _____

Date _____   Term _____

QUANTITY OF WORK   Has the student completed all assignments?

Invention _____   Journal Entries _____

Drafts & Revisions _____   Quizzes _____

Workshop Responses _____   Revision Plans _____

Self-Evaluations _____   Attendance_____

QUALITY OF WORK   To what extent has the student:

Used the Guide to Writing creatively? _____

Revised drafts substantially? _____

Given helpful workshop responses? _____

Written perceptive self-evaluations? _____

Edited and proofread carefully? _____

Used the journal productively? _____

Participated in class discussions? _____

These areas need special attention in the remainder of the course:

MIDTERM GRADE: _____

FINAL COURSE REPORT

Student _____ Course _____

Instructor _____ Section _____

Date _____ Term _____

Remarks on FINAL ESSAY _____

_____

_____

_____

_____

_____

_____

_____

Remarks on WHOLE COURSE _____

_____

_____

_____

_____

_____

_____

_____

_____

_____

_____

FINAL GRADE: _____

STUDENT RECORD FORM

Student _____

Course _____

Section _____

Midterm grade _____   Final grade _____

Assignment	Topic	Invention	Drafts	Critical Comments by	Revision Plan	Revision	Self-Evaluation

Overview and Suggested Course Plans

3

The *Concise Guide* opens with a chapter that addresses the central concerns of this book: why and how we write. This introductory chapter focuses on the writing process, describing it through writers' testimony and offering practical advice on how to manage the process. The rest of the book is divided into the following parts:

OVERVIEW OF THE TEXT

Part One: Writing Activities (Chapters 2–7)

These chapters cover six kinds of nonfiction prose—autobiography, profile, explanatory paper, position paper, proposal, and evaluation. The writing assignments are versatile, producing short or long essays, based on personal experience and observation or on library research. New to this edition are suggestions for writing essays on two thematic strands, "identity and community" and "work and career." Students focusing on one of these strands throughout the course will gain in-depth knowledge in a specific area and will likely be more intellectually engaged with their topics. Each chapter includes the following components:

- Scenarios describing writing in school, in the community, and at work
- Collaborative activities
- Reading selections, each followed by questions for discussion and analysis and by a commentary
- A summary of the basic features of the kind of writing illustrated by the readings
- A writing assignment based on the kind of writing treated in the chapter

- A Guide to Writing that includes strategies for invention and research, planning and drafting, getting critical comments, revising, and editing and proofreading
- An activity to help students think about what they've learned about the writing process

Part Two: Strategies for Writing and Research (Chapters 8–14)

This section offers methods of cueing readers (thesis statements, paragraphing, cohesive devices, and connectives) as well as strategies for invention, such as clustering, listing, cubing, looping, dramatizing, and questioning. The critical reading strategies include annotating, outlining, paraphrasing, summarizing, evaluating the logic of an argument, and recognizing emotional manipulation, among others. New to this edition of the *Concise Guide* are writing strategies for arguing—with numerous exercises and extensive illustrations from professional writers—and techniques for field research. The section also includes techniques for conducting library research and research on the Internet, as well as guidance on using and acknowledging sources following both the Modern Language Association (MLA) and the American Psychological Association (APA) styles.

SUGGESTED COURSE PLANS

The *Concise Guide* is a versatile textbook. It enables you to organize a writing course in many different ways and with quite diverse emphases. With it, you can design a course in which students base their writing solely on personal experience, or one in which they regularly use library resources. You can emphasize critical thinking and reading skills by focusing on the reading selections and their analysis questions along with the guides for critically reading a draft. You can develop a case study course around a problem of general interest by asking students to write reflective, explanatory, and argumentative essays about the same subject. You can help novice writers grasp the fundamentals of written English or challenge experienced writers to stretch their abilities by focusing on stylistic options. You can structure your class around lectures, discussions, workshops, or conferencing.

Here we outline course plans suitable for a fifteen-week semester and a ten-week quarter. These plans are constructed around the major writing assignments in Part One. We assume instructors will integrate material in Part Two into their course plans through reading assignments, classroom activities, and exercise assignments.

You may wish to visit the book companion site at <www.bedfordstmartins .com/conciseguide> for links to additional resources. For information regarding print supplements recommended for use with the *Concise Guide,* see the Introduction to this manual.

Course Plans That Include the Major Types of Writing in Part One

Following are course plans for a single semester and a quarter. For your convenience in reviewing the course plans, here is an outline of Part One that briefly defines each chapter's assignment:

Chapter 2: Remembering Events. Students write a narrative that conveys the significance of a past event.

Chapter 3: Writing Profiles. Students observe and then present people or activities in their community.

Chapter 4: Explaining a Concept. Students investigate a concept and explain it to their readers.

Chapter 5: Arguing a Position. Students examine an issue and present an argument to support their position.

Chapter 6: Proposing a Solution. Students analyze a problem and develop a case for their own solution.

Chapter 7: Justifying an Evaluation. Students establish criteria on which they base an evaluation of something.

The assignments in Part One move from reflective to informative to argumentative forms of writing. The reflective essay—Chapter 2 on remembered events—stresses the exploration of memory and feeling. Students learn to find meaning in personal experience. They also learn to present their experience so that their readers can understand its significance.

The informative essays—Chapters 3 and 4 on the profile and the explanatory paper—shift the focus from the personal to the public. Students learn to gather, analyze, and synthesize information acquired either first- or secondhand by using invention heuristics as well as field and library research strategies (Chapters 12–14). In presenting what they have learned to their readers, students learn to organize and pace the flow of information and ideas so that readers' interest is aroused and sustained.

The argumentative essays—Chapters 5–7—require students not only to gather and analyze information and ideas but to deliberate upon them and to present the results of their deliberation in a carefully reasoned, well-supported argument. The position paper (Chapter 5) introduces students to the special rhetorical demands of argumentation. The proposal (Chapter 6) develops the idea that arguing can be a constructive activity, one that enables groups of people to take action together to solve common problems.

Evaluation (Chapter 7) expands students' reasoning skills and audience awareness and establishes in students' minds the need to build a case on shared assumptions and principles.

Any of the informative and argumentative essays in Part One can be used as the basis of a library-research paper project, large or small. Several documented essays are presented and discussed in Chapters 4–7.

Single-Semester Course Plan

This plan is designed for a fifteen-week semester and features eight different essay assignments, including an oral presentation and a final research paper project. The following materials are also covered: thesis statement and paragraphing strategies (Chapter 8), arguing strategies (Chapter 11), and research strategies in Chapters 12–14. Chapter 12 on Field Research supports the observational and ethnographic research useful for writing a profile and Chapter 13 on Library and Internet Research may be used in explaining a concept as well as in arguing a position, proposing a solution, and justifying an evaluation.

Wk. 1:   Ch. 1 (Introduction) and Ch. 2 (Remembering Events)

Wk. 2:   Ch. 2 (continued)

Wk. 3:   Ch. 3 (Writing Profiles) and Ch. 12 (Field Research)

Wk. 4:   Ch. 3 (continued)

Wk. 5:   Ch. 4 (Explaining a Concept) and Ch. 8 (Cueing the Reader)

Wk. 6:   Ch. 4 (continued)

Wk. 7:   Ch. 4 (continued)

Wk. 8:   Ch. 11 (Arguing) and Ch. 5 (Arguing a Position)

Wk. 9:   Ch. 5 (continued), Ch. 13 (Library and Internet Research), and Ch. 14 (Using and Acknowledging Sources)

Wk. 10: Ch. 5 (continued)

Wk. 11: Ch. 6 (Proposing a Solution)

Wk. 12: Ch. 6 (continued)

Wk. 13: Ch. 7 (Justifying an Evaluation)

Wk. 14: Ch. 7 (continued)

Wk. 15: Ch. 7 (continued)

Single-Quarter Course Plan

This plan, designed for a ten-week quarter, includes four assignments—one reflective, one informational, and two argumentative essays. Other chapters can, of course, be substituted and a particular kind of writing (reflective, for example) could be eliminated altogether.

Wk. 1:   Ch. 1 (Introduction) and Ch. 2 (Remembering Events)

Wk. 2:   Ch. 2 (continued)

Wk. 3:   Ch. 4 (Explaining a Concept) and Ch. 8 (Cueing the Reader)

Wk. 4:   Ch. 4 (continued)

Wk. 5:   Ch. 4 (continued)

Wk. 6:   Ch. 5 (Arguing a Position) and Ch. 11 (Arguing)

Wk. 7:   Ch. 5 (continued)

Wk. 8:   Ch. 7 (Justifying an Evaluation)

Wk. 9:   Ch. 7 (continued)

Wk. 10: Ch. 7 (continued)

Strategies for Teaching Chapters 2–7

4

Each of the six chapters in Part One focuses on a different kind of nonfiction prose that you may have your students write. The chapters all follow the same plan:

Chapter Introduction

- A brief description of the genre and its various uses.

- Writing in Your Other Courses, Writing in the Community, and Writing in the Workplace show examples from diverse contexts in which students are likely to encounter the chapter's genre again.

- Collaborative Activities (one at the beginning of the chapter and another at the Testing Your Choice stage of invention work) enable students to rehearse the writing situation they are beginning to explore and to try out their tentative essay plans on each other.

Readings and Accompanying Activities

- Readings, Analyzing Writing Strategies, and Commentaries indicate the range of writing strategies used to achieve various purposes for particular audiences.

- Connecting to Culture and Experience sections encourage students to discuss a main idea in the reading in terms of their own experiences.

- Considering Topics for Your Own Essay sections start students generating possible topics and speculating about how they might develop them.

Analysis of Purpose and Audience and Summary of Basic Features

- An analysis of Purpose and Audience is followed by a summary of the genre's Basic Features, which provides examples from the readings.

Guide to Writing

- The Guide to Writing escorts students through the process of writing each kind of essay.

- Invention and Research helps students choose a topic and gather the information and ideas needed to write an essay in the genre about their chosen topic.

- Planning and Drafting encourages students to set achievable goals for their draft and to organize their ideas.

- The Critical Reading Guide helps students read each other's drafts critically and constructively.

- Revising and Editing and Proofreading lead students to revise their writing thoughtfully and systematically.

Reflecting on Your Writing

- This section invites students to review their writing process and to recognize that they now have the resources to solve problems they encounter in particular kinds of writing.

In the chapter-by-chapter discussion in Chapter 5 of this manual, we will suggest ways of approaching each individual assignment. Here, we examine each of the components listed above to suggest ways of handling them in the classroom.

CHAPTER INTRODUCTION

Writing in Your Other Courses

Writing in the Community

Writing in the Workplace

Each chapter includes two typical assignments from college courses across the disciplines, from community organizations, and from professional and business situations.

There is much you can do to involve students in analyzing these examples:

- You can analyze one for them, emphasizing all of its thinking/writing demands, and then they can analyze another (either in small groups or as a class).

- You can ask each student to find another assignment in another course.
- You can ask students to bring in examples from organizations or community groups to which they belong.
- You can ask students to bring in examples from their current workplace.
- You can have students do research on the kinds of work or graduate study they are interested in to discover which genres are commonly written in those fields.

A Collaborative Activity

A Collaborative Activity early in each chapter engages students immediately in an interactive, oral rehearsal of the situation they will encounter when they write the chapter's essay assignment.

You'll notice that each collaborative activity is distinctly divided into two parts: first, the rehearsal of the writing situation and, second, a reflection on what happened and what students learned. You may have to help students make this shift. The whole activity need not take more than twenty minutes or so. Because students *experience* the writing situation early in the chapter, we have found they are much more interested in the readings and questions. It starts them into a chapter in a surprisingly productive way. Don't skip this activity!

READINGS AND ACCOMPANYING ACTIVITIES

In each of the chapters of Part One there are three short readings illustrating the kind of writing the chapter presents. Some of the readings are complete essays, while others are edited pieces. Most are by recognized authors, but we have included in each set at least one essay written by a first-year college student using an earlier version of this book.

Each of the readings is followed by these sections:

- Connecting to Culture and Experience: a topic for small-group or whole-class discussion of an idea in the reading
- Analyzing Writing Strategies: two questions for analysis requiring close reading
- Commentary: our brief analysis of an important rhetorical feature of each reading, without answering any of the questions in the Analyzing Writing Strategies section
- Considering Topics for Your Own Essay: suggestions for topics students can consider writing about

Taken together, the Commentary and Analyzing Writing Strategies sections present all of the rhetorical concepts students need to understand and produce the kind of writing treated in the chapter. Moreover, these sections make cross-references to specific writing and research strategies discussed and illustrated in Part Two of the *Concise Guide*.

The following chart indicates some of the Connecting to Culture and Experience and Considering Topics for Your Own Essay sections that are particularly useful for generating ideas about the thematic strands "identity and community" and "work and career."

	Identity and Community	Work and Career
2. Events	Dillard: Connecting Bragg: Connecting	
3. Profiles	"Soup": Considering	"Soup": Connecting
4. Explanation	Toufexis: Connecting	
5. Position	Leshner: Connecting	
6. Proposal		Newman: Connecting; Considering
7. Evaluation	Ansen: Connecting Romano: Connecting	

Readings

We have selected the readings carefully to represent a variety of examples of each kind of writing. They illustrate most of the features and strategies that characterize the type of writing. The readings in each chapter, therefore, work together as a set, and we try to assign as many of them as we can.

The purpose of the readings is to introduce writers to each kind of writing, showing them how various good writing of that kind can look, before they begin their own essays. Novice writers may be encouraged by seeing that other students have trod the way before them and used earlier versions of this book to learn to write.

Readings play an important role in each chapter of this book because we believe that writers benefit from studying good professional writing. We do *not* prescribe the readings as models for students to imitate, but as examples of the many possible directions in which they can take their own writing. A few carefully chosen readings allow us to demonstrate some of the choices available to writers and also to point out the basic features of the type of writing as they appear in each of the readings. We can show students how the readings differ and also what they have in common. We believe that, used carefully, readings can inspire writers rather than intimidate them. Readings help them develop a sense of the problems they must face in each kind of writing and equip them with options for solving these problems.

Connecting to Culture and Experience

A Connecting to Culture and Experience section following each reading lets students engage the ideas in the reading before analyzing it rhetorically. The discussion task is set so that students can connect their personal experience to an idea in the text. It gives students practice in talking about ideas in texts, something few of them do every day, and we believe it increases both their interest in a text and their willingness to analyze it.

We have had excellent results with this follow-up assignment: Immediately after the discussion, students take notes about their ideas; later they draft an extended journal entry; then, at the next class meeting, they share their ideas with members of their discussion group. This activity extends, refines, and clarifies each student's ideas.

Analyzing Writing Strategies

The analysis questions draw students into many different talking and writing activities:

- Locating and identifying features of the reading and strategies the writer has used
- Analyzing the writer's use of these strategies and their effects
- Putting themselves in the writer's position and considering reasons for the writer's choices and solutions to the problems
- Evaluating these choices and solutions and suggesting alternatives and improvements

The analysis questions aim to actively engage students in the readings, leading them to explore beneath the surface of each reading and to examine rhetorical features and strategies they find there. The questions give students practice in thinking about the issues and problems that writers of each kind of writing must address and about the decisions they must make. We find that this helps writers understand what they are trying to do in the assignment. Looking at what other writers have done to see what works and why it works helps them set and pursue achievable and purposeful goals in their own writing.

Commentary

The purpose of the brief commentary on each reading selection is to introduce one or two basic features and strategies illustrated in the reading. The commentaries complement the Analyzing Writing Strategies questions. In many cases, a particular feature or strategy identified in one commentary becomes the subject of a question in subsequent readings. Sometimes an analysis question introduces a feature or strategy that is taken up in the commentary for a later reading. This recursiveness is designed to reinforce students' learning.

The commentaries also introduce concepts discussed in further detail in Part Two. Cross-references have been included where appropriate.

The commentaries are intended to model close rhetorical analysis of the readings and to stimulate further discussion. They are neither exhaustive nor definitive. We expect you and your students to find places where you can extend, illustrate, or disagree with our analysis. The point is to get students thinking and talking about how writing in the genre works. We encourage our students to imagine themselves in the writer's place to speculate about why the writer might have made particular choices. We also urge students to think about the wisdom of those choices and to consider ways in which the essay could be revised.

Using the Readings and Analysis Questions in Class.   The readings and questions are adaptable enough to suit a variety of class plans. To cover all the readings and questions in depth takes up to two class periods and some homework assignments, so in each chapter you may want to concentrate on just one or two of the readings. Another way to save time is to address only one of the questions following each reading.

If you follow the sequence of each chapter, discussion of the readings precedes students' work on invention for their own essays, ensuring that they will have a solid grounding in each kind of writing before they attempt it. They will have read some good examples and thought about the issues raised by the analysis questions. The summary of Basic Features then reviews and consolidates the important issues for each kind of writing, preparing students to begin the invention process.

An alternative scheme would be to have students begin their invention while reading the selections. You could introduce the invention activities by discussing particular readings. If you choose to integrate the invention task with discussion of the readings, the summary of Basic Features section, which follows the readings in each chapter, can be a preview for students before they begin invention and a review before they begin their first drafts. You may also want to save one of the readings—perhaps the student essay—to discuss at this point.

When we discuss the readings in class, we use the analysis questions in two formats: an open forum, with the instructor acting as moderator, or small groups of three or four students, with each group discussing a question about one of the texts. Participation by the whole class allows you to steer the discussion of the readings directly. One good way to ensure that everyone has something to contribute to the discussion is to assign an informal, one-page response to one of the analysis questions as a journal entry, if you have students keep journals. You can then call on some students to read aloud what they have written. This response can be written as homework before the class, or it can be written in five or ten minutes at the beginning of the class period.

These short written responses to the analysis questions can also help to initiate discussion in small groups, with one student in each group reading his or her response to the others in the group. In large classes this format allows more students to participate, and it can elicit responses from students who would not speak in front of the whole class. After ten or fifteen minutes, a student from each group can make a brief oral summary of the group's discussion for the rest of the class. These summaries can naturally lead into a whole-class discussion of the readings or a brief lecture by the instructor on some specific writing issue that appears in the readings.

Successful Class Discussions of the Readings.   Since the primary purpose of discussing the readings is to help students write essays of the same kind, we make frequent connections between the features we find in the readings and those that students will be generating in their invention writing. We usually make these connections as we summarize the main points of the discussion. Often we summarize by listing discourse features and strategies on the chalkboard, inviting students to help us make the lists. Students then have a visual reminder of the key points they are learning, and the instructor can happily avoid the role of Inspector of Responses in favor of being the leader and recorder of the discussion.

In our most successful class discussions, the students do most of the talking and talk to each other rather than just to us. The best discussions also have momentum: Students are able to sustain discussion instead of merely answering our questions. This is why the analysis questions focus on important writing issues but do not ask students simply for facts. We intend for the questions to open up discussion and engage students in the problems they will be facing in their own essays, not merely to test their comprehension of the readings.

Considering Topics for Your Own Essay

This section anticipates the first invention step in the Guide to Writing: listing topics and choosing one. Even before they arrive at invention, students begin generating possible topics and considering the possibilities and constraints of the assignment. If they read all three readings and consider the writing possibilities following each one, they will be well prepared to identify their own essay topics.

You can profitably approach this activity as an occasion for whole-class brainstorming. Each student can contribute at least one topic and speculate about its appeal and requirements. You can then single out topics that seem especially promising. Each student can then take any topic and rehearse it briefly in writing.

ANALYSIS OF PURPOSE AND AUDIENCE AND BASIC FEATURES

Between the Readings and the Guide to Writing sections, each chapter contains a discussion of the rhetorical possibilities and a summary of the basic features for that kind of writing. The Purpose and Audience section draws students' attention to the rhetoric of the selections and helps them think about their own purposes and potential readers. The Basic Features section summarizes the main points raised in the readings by the analysis questions and the commentaries, thus giving students a chance to review and consolidate the information they have learned so far before trying to apply it in their own essays. If students understand the basic features of each kind of writing and have seen how they work in the readings, it should be easier for them to respond to the invention tasks. Student writers often have difficulty coming up with much useful material until they learn the value of the features that the invention tasks ask them to generate. Referring students to the Purpose and Audience and Basic Features sections during the composing process reminds them of the key rhetorical issues for their writing.

GUIDE TO WRITING

The Guide to Writing assists the student in learning how to write the genre under consideration. Each Guide to Writing is tailored to consider special challenges the student will meet during the writing process. The following discussion presents overall advice and specific teaching strategies for these sections in the Guides to Writing: Invention and Research, Planning and Drafting, Critical Reading Guide, Revising, and Editing and Proofreading.

Invention and Research

Each Guide includes a sequence of invention activities designed specifically to help students ask themselves questions and generate ideas and information useful for their essays. Since so few students have ever participated in systematic invention, we are especially careful to introduce them to the invention activities. We ask the students to open their books to the invention section and then briefly explain the purpose of each activity. By having students turn the pages and skim the invention exercises while you preview them orally, you will be able to reduce students' apprehension about these unfamiliar activities and greatly increase the probability that they will successfully complete the invention section before beginning their drafts.

This is also the time to remind students of the time frame for invention: Suggest that they begin work right away but spread the work out over several sessions; tell them what day the invention will be due, and that you will be checking it on that day to ensure that their invention base is adequate to begin planning and drafting.

The first part of the invention asks students to list possible subjects and includes suggestions for general topics as well as for specific ones drawn from two thematic strands, "identity and community" and "work and career." You could do part of the invention in class as whole-class brainstorming or in small groups, beginning by reading the lists in the book and moving to other topics the students can think of. Students then move to choosing a topic and exploring it. Students will progress through the invention sequence at different rates, but you can help them stay on track by requiring them to reach a certain point by a certain class meeting. If you ask them to bring their invention in progress to every class meeting, you can ask them to share certain sections with their peers in pairs or small groups while you circulate and examine each student's work to date.

Research is comfortably included in our broad definition of invention — everything that happens before and during writing to produce ideas and evaluate them. Except for the writing activities in Chapter 2 on reflective writing, all the other writing activities (Chapters 3 through 7) can include formal research. In our discussion about how to teach these activities (in Chapter 5 of this manual), we explain how students can complete these assignments either with or without formal research. For example, depending on their topics, students can explain a concept that they already know without using or documenting any sources, or they can research new topics, relying entirely on sources (Chapter 4: Explaining a Concept).

Where research is appropriate, the Guide to Writing invites it. You can decide how much research students should do, or leave it to them to decide. We provide additional guidance in Chapter 12: Strategies for Field Research, Chapter 13: Strategies for Library and Internet Research, and Chapter 14: Strategies for Using and Acknowledging Sources.

Planning and Drafting

The Planning and Drafting section in each chapter in Part One is organized as follows:

- Seeing What You Have
- Setting Goals (focused on each chapter's type of writing)
- Outlining
- Drafting

Invention may produce a number of complete paragraphs, several lists, freewriting, an interview, or notes on library research — a plethora of material that must be organized before the student can write a draft. This much material poses a new problem for many students: what to do with all of it.

The Guide to Writing in each chapter urges students to consider several alternative plans before settling on one. Often students are unaware of alternatives; we find it helpful to illustrate several, sometimes from the reading selections and sometimes from topics suggested by students.

Each planning section reminds students, as they go on to draft, that what they have developed is only a plan; in other words, it is expendable. The final test for the paper is not whether it follows the outline, but whether it works. Like many other parts of the Guide to Writing, this may demand from inexperienced writers a new approach, a new order of priorities.

Up to the drafting stage, the student has been dealing with pieces or facets; now for the first time the student will attempt to see the material as a whole. We suggest that students write their first rough drafts in a single sitting lasting about two to three hours. The drafting session resembles extended freewriting. It lasts longer, it allows the student to pause much more, and of course the writer is trying for a more ordered product; but, as in freewriting, the writer should work as fast as possible and not worry too much about grammatical details or spelling.

The object of this approach is to keep the student focused on the larger shape of the essay, not on distracting details. Research shows that most competent writers occasionally write garbled sentences in their first drafts and that writers who struggle to perfect each sentence as it is written are inefficient. Of course, there are exceptions, and students should remember that the Guide to Writing is just that—a guide, not a set of inflexible orders.

Critical Reading Guide

The part of this section called the Critical Reading Guide assists students in analyzing a classmate's draft. Like the invention sequence, this section is specific to the particular genre. Nevertheless, in the various chapters these guides follow a general pattern. First the student reads the draft straight through and gives a general impression in just a few sentences. During close reading and rereading, the student analyzes the discourse features and strategies of the particular kind of writing being worked on. This section consists of several close-reading tasks that ask the student to *describe* and *evaluate* the draft. The tasks mirror the discourse issues central to the readings, questions, and commentaries at the beginning of each chapter, the summary of Basic Features, the invention activities, and the advice on drafting. This circling back again and again to the central rhetorical issues for a genre emphasizes the recursiveness of the writing process in each chapter. Attentive students who have come this far—and who are able to analyze their own and other students' drafts thoughtfully—are in a surprisingly strong position to produce a solid revision.

Students may use the analysis section in various ways: (1) to guide an in-class written analysis of another student's draft; (2) to guide an at-home written analysis of another student's draft, to prepare for a conference or class discussion, or just to turn over the analysis to the other student; and (3) to guide their discussions of drafts in pairs, in small groups, or in a whole-class workshop.

We recommend starting with a written analysis. To eliminate problems of duplicating and exchanging papers in advance of class meetings, we schedule class time for a written analysis of each draft. Then we move on to some form of talk about the drafts. (See Organizing Workshops in Chapter 1: Teaching Practices in this manual.) Students need fifteen to twenty-five minutes to complete a thorough analysis, though, of course, you could ask for a quicker analysis.

The written analysis—as homework or in class—adds still another piece of writing to the class, writing of a type generally different from the essay the student is working on. It holds students' attention closely to the written text as they search for evidence to substantiate their evaluations. It is a writing-to-learn exercise par excellence, requiring review and use of the discourse concepts presented in the chapter. We have found that it also produces better workshop discussions of drafts.

In each chapter, before students use the Critical Reading Guide, we recommend that you orient them to it carefully, even take them through each step to ensure that they understand how to read and respond to the draft. Encourage them to write as much as they can, to be as specific as possible without worrying about being right or straining to say something wise. Each student should just try to give a full response as one thoughtful reader.

These peer critiques not only make it possible for every student to receive some reaction to a rough draft before revising, but they also help teach students the critical reading techniques they need to use on their own papers. With coaching and practice, students can write apt, detailed, and insightful criticism. As they realize their own successes, students will come to respect both themselves and their classmates as readers and helpers. This respect improves every other classroom activity; most particularly, it does wonders for small-group work, when students must look to each other rather than to the teacher for help or ideas.

Revising

This section has a revising plan that is organized as follows:

- Getting an Overview
- Carrying Out Revisions

Students are now on their own, perhaps with advice from other students and from you, to improve their drafts. Carrying Out Revisions takes them back through the possibilities of the assignment they are working on. It gives very specific advice about how they can solve problems they recognize in their drafts.

It will be an excellent use of class time to ask students to make or at least begin their plan for revision under your guidance. If they are able to reread their drafts carefully, compose a scratch outline, and study their peers' comments while they are in the classroom with you available to answer questions, they will be well launched into the process and able to complete it and then revise their drafts on their own. Alternatively, students could write out their revision plans outside of class and you could review them at the next class meeting to ensure that they're on track. Then you could select and duplicate the best revision plan and ask the writer to present it to the class as a model.

Editing and Proofreading

The last step in revising is editing and proofreading—checking a draft at the sentence level and correcting errors in grammar, punctuation, and mechanics. We ask students to keep a record of the types of errors they habitually make and to check their writing for these errors. (See Responding to Error in Chapter 2: Evaluation Practices in this manual.)

REFLECTING ON YOUR WRITING

Coming at the end of the chapter, after students have written and edited their final revisions, this section may seem to be merely an afterthought. But in our teaching, it has become an integral part of students' work in each kind of writing they do in Part One. This writing activity brings closure to students' work in the chapter. It reinforces what students have learned about solving problems in their writing.

We routinely ask students to write a page or so as part of the package (invention writing, drafts, etc.) they hand in with the final revision of each essay. Because students sometimes view this activity as make-work, we usually spend some class time discussing why we require it. You could have students write their explanations in class on the day the final revision is handed in and then devote part of the class to discussing what students wrote.

When we grade and respond to the revised essay, we make a point of referring to the students' own reflections on how they discovered and tried to solve a particular problem in their writing. If their solution doesn't work very well, for example, we may be able to suggest other ways of reworking the essay. Often we can offer some additional ideas on how they can avoid the problem in the future. Sometimes we point out another problem and invite the student to revise the essay one more time, trying to solve that particular problem. We might also refer students to strategies used in one or two of the readings that they might be able to adapt to their purposes.

We also find students' written reflections useful for periodic conferences and for midterm class discussions. Often in conference we can suggest specific ways a student could use the invention activities to avoid a recurrent kind of problem or the strategies in the readings to solve the problem. Midterm discussion with the entire class could reinforce students' images of themselves as problem-solvers, capable of learning from reading as well as from others.

Detailed Chapter Plans

5

This section will guide you through the chapters in numerical sequence and provide detailed information about each. As the overall structure of the Part One chapters (Chapters 2 through 7) has already been explored in Chapter 4 of this manual, here we focus instead on ways of approaching each of the six writing assignments. For those chapters which we have not yet explored in great detail—namely, the introductory chapter (Chapter 1) and the chapters in Part Two (Chapters 8 through 14), we briefly outline the structure and provide suggestions for teaching the exercises.

CHAPTER 1: INTRODUCTION

This brief introductory chapter begins by arguing that writing makes important contributions to thinking, learning, success, personal development, and communication. It then explains how writing is learned: how written texts work, how the writing process works, and how to think critically about writing. Each section in this chapter discusses how we can learn what we need to know and includes one or two exercises that could be used along with the quotations as the basis for class discussion.

In Reading, we introduce the concepts of purpose, audience, and genre or kind of writing. These are concepts central to the writing assignment chapters in Part One, each of which focuses on a different genre. We define genres as social acts: Different rhetorical situations call for different genres. We talk about the predictability as well as the variability of genres. The point is that genres have conventions, patterns that help readers understand them, but they should not be thought of as formulaic or static. By placing genres in their social context, we can see how they reflect as well as affect the values and assumptions of the people who use them.

The next section, Writing, introduces the idea that writing is a complex and recursive process. We refer here to writing as creative problem-solving, a notion that we come back to at the end of each Part One chapter, in Reflecting on Your Writing. We also introduce the important idea that writing is not always a solitary activity, but often involves collaboration. Since the

Concise Guide offers many opportunities for collaboration, you might want to reinforce this idea by putting students into small discussion groups and having them exchange the metaphors and similes they've thought of for Exercise 1.5.

We also introduce the Guides to Writing in each of the Part One chapters. The Guides, as we explain, provide procedural scaffolding to help students recognize the full potential of the writing process. They help students resist the impulse to be done even before they've begun exploring their topic. They also make the process somewhat less imposing by suggesting how students might break it into smaller, more focused tasks.

Exercise 1.4 could be used to get students to reflect on what they typically do when they write. Many students will say they are satisfied with the process they currently use, even if that involves what we've called the "dangerous method." The Guides to Writing try to increase students' repertoire of strategies for invention, planning, revising, and editing. They offer an array of heuristic questions specific to the genre that encourages students to think more about their subject as well as to think more systematically.

Students also need to know how to think critically about their writing. What we are talking about here is metacognition—thinking about thinking. There's ample evidence to suggest that learners learn better when they reflect on what they are learning. Conscious reflection also seems to help writers in the process of writing. As Linda Flower points out in "Taking Thought: The Role of Conscious Processing in the Making of Meaning," writers can often rely on strategies they have used many times before. But when the subject is especially challenging or they are writing in a genre that is new to them, writers—no matter how expert—shift to a heightened state of awareness so that they can use all of the resources at their command.

The section called Using This Book forecasts the plan of the book, emphasizing the Guides to Writing in the writing assignment chapters of Part One. Some general advice about invention, drafting, revising, and editing concludes the chapter.

CHAPTER 2: REMEMBERING EVENTS
THE WRITING ASSIGNMENT

Write an essay about an event in your life that will be engaging for readers and that will, at the same time, help them understand the significance of the event. Tell your story dramatically and vividly.

The Nature of the Writing Assignment

This assignment has several goals: to teach students to write a meaningful narrative and to introduce the rhetorical concepts of purpose and audience. This chapter presents the basic strategies of effective storytelling. Students learn how to sequence the action chronologically, to shape the structure of their narratives meaningfully, and to use a consistent point of view.

By focusing the writing assignment on the significance of the event, the chapter draws students' attention to the way in which purpose and audience control the selection as well as the presentation of details. Students writing about significant events must decide how they want to present themselves. This assignment involves students, sometimes for the first time, in reflecting seriously about their own experience. It encourages students to make discoveries about themselves and to share these insights with others through writing. For inexperienced writers, this use of writing as discovery can lead to an important new commitment to writing, a commitment that subsequent assignments attempt to foster.

Autobiographical writing is treated here not merely as an exercise in storytelling, but as a meaningful intellectual activity. In learning about autobiographical writing, students discover the basic process of all writing—making meaning from experience. That is, they learn how to present their experiences so that readers can understand what has happened and why it is important.

Many instructors like to begin writing courses with a unit on reflective writing, writing that relies on the invention strategies of memory search and analysis as well as the writing strategies of narration and description. We open with autobiography because it enables students to use a fairly straightforward narrative organization for their essays.

Special Problems of This Writing Assignment

We have noticed that students facing this assignment for the first time may have problems developing an engaging narrative and revealing the event's significance.

In their first drafts of essays about events, student writers tend to draw on what they know of storytelling conventions. Typically this involves beginning with a general introduction that sets the scene or declares the significance of the event in broad terms. The succession of events is then played out in the body of the paper without much alteration in pace to include descriptive details, the writer's feelings at the time, and reflections with hindsight. A writer often forgets to show as well as tell, to bring an experience alive with sensory detail rather than merely record the sequence of events.

Many writers have initial difficulties managing the pace of a narrative, not realizing that the climax of an event can easily be undercut if pages of incidental events have misdirected readers' expectations. We find it useful to spend some time explaining ways to adjust the flow of time and create suspense. As the commentaries show, the readings offer good examples of ways to order and shape narratives.

For many writers, the companion to the convention of beginning a story with a general introduction is the convention of ending it with a moral. Unused to probing the personal significance of events they write about, inexperienced writers tend to translate this convention into a moralistic conclusion. Again we use the readings to point out ways in which reflection on the significance of an event can be woven into the narrative and how to avoid simplistic conclusions. We encourage them to go deeper—to look at reasons for their actions and reactions, to explore the humorous or absurd possibilities of their topics and the personal insights that these can provide.

Promising and Unpromising Topics

The writing assignment in this chapter gives students a wide choice of topics. This latitude, as students soon discover, presents problems as well as opportunities. The chief problem comes when students choose events from which they do not have enough distance or events in which the significance is too obvious.

When asked to choose a significant event, students frequently want to write about the first topic that comes to mind, often a recent or traumatic experience. An event that happened very recently may only appear to be important because it is on the writer's mind. While writing about such an event will help the writer understand it, the event may turn out not to have much meaning after all. Traumatic events may also be problematic as topics, not because they lack significance but because they are too meaningful. Writing about a traumatic event may involve more self-disclosure than seems appropriate given the writing situation.

Looking back over the events of their lives for possible topics, writers understandably tend to think big. Major emotional landmarks readily come to mind: graduation, making the team, having an accident, passing or failing the big test. In the Guide to Writing, we suggest that students also consider events from other categories, including topics from the "identity and community" and "work and career" strands.

Some of the peak experiences we suggest are initiations or rites of passage. They are prominent in the minds of many students and can make excellent autobiographical topics. The events featured in all the readings in this chapter may also be said to involve rites of passage.

A problem, however, with these topics is that many of them are common experiences, familiar to almost everyone. The challenge in writing about such an event is to avoid the cliché, to find something distinctive in the experience, or to give readers a new perspective on it. We encourage students to think twice before writing about their first experience on the ski slopes, the prom that was not all it promised to be, the event that would have embarrassed anyone. Experiences such as these that exactly match expectations contain nothing surprising for readers, no new insights or discoveries. Students would do better to look beyond the obvious and consider some of the subtler experiences they may have had—moments of intense awareness, realizations, important changes that took place within themselves.

CHAPTER INTRODUCTION

Writing in Your Other Courses

Writing in the Community

Writing in the Workplace

We wouldn't want to overemphasize the number of times students will be asked to write about their personal experience in their college courses, in their communities, or at work. In fact, you may want to take this opportunity to discuss with them the value of writing about personal experience. First-year students, both the eighteen-year-old variety and the older student, are often struck by the abstractness of their college studies. Some instructors may appear to disdain self-examination (even though Socrates taught us that the unexamined life is not worth living). The examples of college writing assignments and the descriptions of community and job-related writing situations suggest the role of personal experience in our understanding of ourselves and of the society in which we live and work.

Practice Remembering an Event: A Collaborative Activity

If you decide to have your students do this collaborative activity, you will find that their interest in the chapter will be enhanced, along with their confidence that they will be able to write an interesting remembered event essay. This activity guides them through a rehearsal for the essay they will write later and prepares them to think seriously about the genre.

If you are beginning the course with this chapter, this particular collaborative activity provides a good starting point. It has students tell each other stories, which is always fun. And it gives students a chance to get to know one another and begin to form a good working relationship.

READINGS

All of the readings in this chapter involve childhood experiences. That is not to say, of course, that students must be limited in their own topic choice. But since most students using this book are still quite young and relatively inexperienced, we thought the focus on childhood would have the widest appeal. We also wanted to give instructors an opportunity to compare and contrast the readings' themes.

One recurrent theme in autobiography appears to be the struggle to acquire a sense of identity, to define one's self. All the writers in this chapter contend with this issue. Dillard's self-definition hinges on her discovery of pursuits that are hers alone. She assumes her parents care about what she's been doing in the basement and is at first surprised and then relieved to find that they are basically uninterested. Bragg explores his attempts to achieve social status in his small-town high school through his possession of a powerful car. And Brandt, the student author in the collection, comes to understand herself and her relationship with her parents after shoplifting an inexpensive button.

Other themes are suggested in the Connecting to Culture and Experience and Considering Topics for Your Own Essay sections following each reading, and you will undoubtedly see still other thematic connections worth making.

Topics in Analysis Questions and Commentaries

These lists can serve as a quick reference to help you plan your discussion of discourse features either in class or in conference.

Dillard, "Handed My Own Life"	
Analyzing Writing Strategies	*Commentary: Organizing a Well-Told Story*
1. features of a remembered event essay	narrative organization
2. naming and detailing	specific narrative action
Bragg, "100 Miles per Hour, Upside Down and Sideways"	
Analyzing Writing Strategies	*Commentary: Autobiographical Significance*
1. comparing	showing and telling
2. incident	dominant impression
Brandt, "Calling Home"	
Analyzing Writing Strategies	*Commentary: A Vivid Presentation of Places and People*
1. dialogue	dialogue: summarizing and quoting
2. framing	

Handed My Own Life Anne Dillard

Dillard's story might surprise some students because it is not particularly dramatic, and it is certainly not traumatic or even disturbing. Students need to realize that to be significant an experience does not have to be earth-shattering, nor does it have to be sad. Dillard writes about a liberating experience, one that helped make her the confident, independent, hard-working person she has become.

The questions ask students to consider why Dillard wrote this piece and what she wanted readers to think of her after reading it. This issue of self-presentation goes to the heart of writing autobiography and may be relevant to the very act of writing. It is especially pertinent for students who are concerned about exposing themselves to their classmates and their instructor.

Connecting to Culture and Experience: Coming of Age

This activity, which might be handled in small groups or by the class as a whole, is designed to get students thinking about the significance of Dillard's remembered event. We want students to understand that autobiographical writing is not only personal, but also has a social dimension. It connects the writer's and readers' experiences and says something about what people value and how their values may be in conflict—even within themselves.

The instructions lead students from the specific to the general. They focus students' attention on the writer's perspective and ask them to compare it to their own. We basically want students to consider two issues: How might seemingly trivial experiences shape one's identity? And what cultural values and attitudes inform these experiences? This activity also invites students to speculate on the importance of events in their own lives that may seem trivial, but that actually may have some larger significance in terms of their growth as individuals or as members of specific communities.

Analyzing Writing Strategies

1. This question asks students to examine Dillard's essay in light of what we've said about the aims and characteristics of remembered event essays. By looking closely at Dillard's essay both for what is and is not there, students can get a better understanding of what this kind of writing tries to accomplish.

2. The aim of this question is to draw students' attention to Dillard's visual descriptions and to emphasize the importance of this writing strategy in remembered event essays.

Commentary: Organizing a Well-Told Story

This commentary concentrates on the dramatic structure of Dillard's essay, which covers a few months of her childhood, leading up to the significant realization about herself and her relationship to her parents. We provide a scratch outline that shows the simple chronology of the essay. Students will notice that the actual sighting of the amoeba does not occur until the seventh paragraph. As we point out, though, only action and information that set up the dramatic sighting are included in the first six paragraphs, which arouse our curiosity and build suspense. Since students sometimes have difficulty focusing on a specific event that is part of a longer period of their lives, you might want to examine closely the way in which Dillard selects key information to build suspense in the first half of the essay.

The commentary also notes Dillard's strategic use of specific narrative action—active verbs and modifying phrases and clauses—to vividly communicate the way the characters in her story talk, move, and act.

Considering Topics for Your Own Essay

Here students are invited to respond to Dillard's essay by recalling related events in their own lives, when they made a significant discovery or learned something important. You could ask them to first focus on academic sorts of learning, but to then go on to other kinds of learning—learning about oneself, about others, about how to get along in the world. You might encourage students to return to this section—and similar sections in the following readings—when they begin the invention process.

| *100 Miles Per Hour* |
| Rick Bragg |

In this excerpt from Bragg's autobiography, he writes about an experience that will be familiar to many students: working to buy a car that becomes a status symbol for him and miraculously escaping death when he wrecks it. Bragg's essay, like Dillard's, covers an extended period of time, building suspense for and leading up to a single dramatic event. We direct students' attention to the opening metaphor, which effectively forecasts the incident.

Connecting to Culture and Experience: Social Status

Whether students are recent high school graduates or older, they will identify with Bragg's attempts to establish his social status among his peers. To prepare them for small-group discussion, you might have students write about their own high school experiences in a journal entry. You might also discuss their answers to the final question, concerning the role of social status in adult relationships, with the entire class.

Analyzing Writing Strategies

1. Students will have different opinions about which metaphor or simile is most effective and which is most vivid. The goal of this question is to help them recognize and articulate comparing functions in good writing. This question can serve as the basis for a small-group activity or an out-of-class assignment. In class, each group could analyze a paragraph and report their findings to the class as a whole.

2. This question, like the commentary on Dillard's essay, focuses on dramatic structure, on how the writer arouses curiosity and builds suspense. By dividing the essay into three sections—context, incident, and conclusion—students will learn how a writer sets up and presents a significant event. Students will notice that although paragraphs 1–8 cover an extended period of time, with references as far back as the summer before the incident, Bragg nonetheless prepares us for the final race.

You might work through the question with the whole class, outlining the incident together. Here is a possible paragraph-by-paragraph scratch outline of this section of the essay:

- Begins the incident with his answer to Kyle Smith's challenge
- Reacts to seeing the police car
- Reveals the consequences of the accident, which he learned at a later point
- Describes his immediate reaction to the accident
- Describes his rescue from the car
- Quotes the state trooper
- Describes his encounter with his mother
- Describes the immediate outcome of the accident

Commentary: Autobiographical Significance

In this commentary, we focus on the ways in which Bragg conveys the autobiographical significance of the event. We distinguish between showing to create a dominant impression and telling what the significance might be, and we point out that Bragg does relatively little telling. Students are also encouraged to see the distinctions between Bragg's remembered thoughts and feelings and his present perspective on his experience. Bragg is writing about this high school event when he is in his mid-thirties, so he has gained some distance from the experience and can differentiate between his adolescent and adult perspectives.

You might use this opportunity to stress the importance of students' choosing events from which they have some distance. The invention activities in Reflecting on the Event's Significance ask students to explore their own past and present perspectives, and you might refer back to this commentary and to Bragg's essay when students begin these activities.

Considering Topics for Your Own Essay

In this question, students are asked to reflect on an incident from a time in their lives upon which they now have, hopefully, more perspective than they do on recent incidents from their teen years—preoccupied as they may be with that era. Encourage students to focus on the change this incident caused in them, and on the contrast between their present and former selves.

Calling Home Jean Brandt

This selection is written by a first-year college student about an event that occurred when she was thirteen. Brandt is writing about an embarrassing event with a good deal of honesty. By focusing on what she felt at the time of the event, Brandt avoids the predictable moral about crime not paying. She boldly presents her changing feelings: naive optimism, humiliation, excitement, shame, worry, relief.

Connecting to Culture and Experience: Shame

Students may be hesitant to speak openly about some occasion that made them feel ashamed, especially if the remembered event essay is the first assignment of the course and they have not established working relationships with their classmates. This activity might work best if students form small groups. You might instruct them to write briefly about such an occasion on a piece of paper that they need not share with others. Then they may reveal as much about the occasion as they feel comfortable revealing.

Analyzing Writing Strategies

1. Brandt uses dialogue throughout this essay: a brief exchange with her sister (end of paragraph 3 and beginning of 4), a summarized dialogue with the man from the store in paragraph 6, an extended exchange with her sister in paragraphs 7–15, a summary of what the police officers said to her in paragraphs 16 and 18, the phone conversation with her father and mother in paragraphs 19–34, and the final comment by her father (and silence by her mother) in paragraphs 36–38.

   Students tend to be insightful about this parent-child relationship. Some will note that the father's anger is more open than the mother's reaction, and that he displaces the blame, converting his daughter into a victim of the authorities. As a victim, Brandt may consider herself freed from taking responsibility. Her mother, however, expresses disappointment and then appears to withdraw her love. When Brandt writes in paragraph 9 about anticipating explaining to her parents, she focuses on her dread of her mother's reaction. Perhaps this is because she knows her mother will respond by withdrawing love. Students familiar with the concept of "tough love" may interpret the mother's reaction positively.

2. The strategy of framing an essay is simple but quite useful. Students will see that the story begins and ends with a car ride. You might ask them to contrast these two scenes. Many readers sense that not only was this experience sobering, but it also helped Brandt mature. In the opening scene she seems to be childish, and in the end she is much more reserved and chastened. You might ask them what Brandt seems to have learned at the time, and what she learned years later from writing about this remembered event.

Commentary: A Vivid Presentation of People and Places

This commentary focuses on Brandt's use of dialogue, on her choices to summarize or quote her own words and those of others. Student writers often hesitate to quote and instead rely exclusively on summary. Others often fail to discriminate between more significant and less significant quotations and instead write narratives that seem more like movie scripts. In this commentary, we also explain the conventions associated with the use of dialogue.

Considering Topics for Your Own Essay

The focus here is on actions that are atypical, times when students did something that surprised even them. We stress that these do not have to be negative experiences. In fact, many are likely to be quite positive, even liberating.

PURPOSE AND AUDIENCE

This section of the chapter reminds students that essays about remembered events have important rhetorical constraints. You might want to discuss the various motives autobiographers have for writing about their own experiences. A way to begin is by asking students about their own choices. Why are they willing to share some memories and not others? How much is their choice affected by their assumptions about readers?

In the reading selections, for example, Dillard presents herself and her parents in the rosiest possible light. Yet even this picture of middle-class domestic bliss can be interpreted another way, for example, as an expression of Dillard's isolation from her parents and her desire for their approval. Many students are surprised that Brandt chose to relate an embarrassing experience like breaking the law and being arrested. One wonders what to make of her obvious pride when she thinks she has successfully stolen the Snoopy button. Is she writing to confess her guilt, to brag, or both? Writers frequently have multiple and even contradictory motives. We want to show our weaknesses but be liked in spite of them, or even because of them.

BASIC FEATURES: REMEMBERING EVENTS

This section reviews the most important features of writing about autobiographically significant events:

- A well-told story
- A vivid presentation of places and people
- An indication of the event's significance

We discuss these features and illustrate them with specific references to the selections.

You might want to discuss them before students plan and draft their own essays, and to review them again before they read each other's drafts, to see how well they used and developed these features in their own writing.

GUIDE TO WRITING

Invention

We recommend the following invention activities to help students choose a promising subject and probe it fully:

- Finding an event to write about
- Describing the place

- Recalling key people
- Sketching the story
- Testing your choice
- Exploring memorabilia
- Reflecting on the event's significance
- Defining your purpose for your readers
- Formulating a tentative thesis statement

We designed this sequence of invention activities to address the special problems that the assignment poses: choosing an appropriate event with autobiographical significance and telling a vivid, engaging story about it.

We offer a list of topics (in the Aristotelian sense)—kinds of events students might consider writing about. The Considering Topics for Your Own Essay section after each reading can also help them think of topics.

Once they have an event to work with, the guide invites them to recall specific sensory details and key people associated with it. These heuristics lead writers to imaginatively recreate the scene, inhabited with people and echoing with language. The idea is that this reenactment will allow them to gain insight into the event's significance. They then sketch out the story and test their choices, in part by rehearsing them for others in their group.

Next we suggest that students collect memorabilia to help flesh out their invention notes and to possibly include in their essays. In the next section, we provide a set of heuristics designed to get them to systematically probe the event's significance. They try to recall their feelings at the time of the experience and contrast these remembered feelings with their present perspective. We find that this procedure, when performed thoughtfully, can be enormously powerful. It enables the writer to create the remembered self as the subject of discourse, often freeing the writer to present the thick texture of experience. We also ask students to focus their thoughts for their specific audience. Finally, we suggest that students write out two or three sentences that state the significance of the event. We advise them that these sentences need not appear in their essays, that they will more likely implicitly show the significance through their narratives.

Testing Your Choice: A Collaborative Activity

Here students are urged to meet with other students to rehearse their stories. Trying out the story in this informal way can help students get a better sense of how to structure the narrative to make it interesting to readers. It also helps them decide whether their choices are good ones.

Planning and Drafting

You might help students plan their essays by conferencing with them about the goals they've set for the essay. In this conference, the student would do most of the talking. Your role would be primarily to help students clarify their global goals—those dealing with purpose and audience.

Critical Reading Guide

This section provides a guide that will help students read each other's drafts and respond constructively. Question 1 directs the reader to get an overall sense of the essay before looking at its basic features.

You will notice that questions 2 through 4 deal with the basic features. We don't expect students to point to everything we mention or to answer every question. They should focus on the areas that seem to them to need special attention. Or the writer could ask the reader to focus on certain questions.

Revising

These sections urge students to think of revising as problem-solving. Analyzing specific features and considering readers' critical comments can help students focus on the aspects of the essay that need substantial revision. The idea of revising as problem-solving is addressed in the concluding section, Reflecting on Your Writing.

Editing and Proofreading

In this section, we direct students to proofread their essays and edit for sentence-level errors. You might ask them to edit and proofread outside of class, or in class with your guidance. This is an appropriate time to discuss grammar and mechanics, with individual students or the class as a whole, within the context of their own writing.

REFLECTING ON YOUR WRITING

Because we have found that students' experience with each genre is made richer through retrospective examination, each assignment chapter in the text concludes with an activity for guided reflection on the students' writing experiences. Having just come through what they may consider an arduous writing process, students may need your special encouragement to approach this activity thoughtfully before moving on to their next assignment.

RESPONDING TO ESSAYS ABOUT REMEMBERED EVENTS

Here are some of the kinds of problems you can expect to find in students' writing about remembered events:

Subject

- The essay does not meet the criteria for an event essay, but seems more like a person essay, reflections essay, or some other type of writing.
- The topic is too broad ("my childhood," "our championship season").
- The event does not seem important to the writer.
- The essay either trivializes a major event or overstates a minor one (this second case can be effective if handled humorously).

Narrative Structure of the Event

- The event sprawls out over too much time or space.
- The event is not clearly framed for the reader; it should begin or end at another point.
- The narrative drags in places, or skims important episodes.
- The narrative lacks dramatic tension or suspense.
- The dialogue is undramatic and uninteresting; it does not move the action forward.

Anecdotes and Scenes

- They are either too brief, or much too extended.
- They do not seem to relate well to the event; they are either poorly chosen or badly framed.
- The essay lacks telling details to build a dominant impression.
- The writer has not selected relevant details, or includes too many trivial, irrelevant ones.
- People do not seem believable in their actions or dialogue.

Significance to the Writer

- There is no apparent significance, stated or implied.
- The significance is heavy-handed, inflated, oversimplified, or sentimentalized; the writer moralizes about the event.
- The essay is not very thoughtful in exploring the event's significance; the writer may come off as a hero or a blameless victim.
- The essay has not given the reader a vivid impression of the writer.

PREPARING FOR CONFERENCES

If you hold conferences with your students on their drafts, you could have them prepare for the conference by filling in the form on the following page.

PREPARING FOR A CONFERENCE: CHAPTER 2

Before the conference, write answers to the questions below. Bring your invention writing and first draft to the conference.

1. Briefly describe the event you are writing about. How did you come to choose it? Why is it important in your life?

2. List the scenes (locations) and people in your essay. Be prepared to talk about which ones are most vividly presented and which may need further or less detailing.

3. Explain briefly how you organized your telling of this event. What other possibilities could you consider for beginning, ending, and organizing the essay?

4. Event essays involve both self-discovery and self-presentation. What, if anything, has writing this draft led you to discover about yourself? What kind of self does your draft now present to readers?

5. What are you most pleased with in this draft? Be specific.

6. What specifically do you need to do next to revise your draft? List any problems you see in the draft or problems that another reader has pointed out. Say briefly how you might attempt to solve these problems. Use the back of this form for these notes. (If you have completed the text's Revising plan, bring it with you to the conference instead of answering this question.)

CHAPTER 3: WRITING PROFILES

THE WRITING ASSIGNMENT

Write an essay about an intriguing person, place, or activity in your community. Observe your subject closely, and then present what you have learned in a way that both informs and engages readers.

The Nature of the Writing Assignment

A profile is an informative and entertaining report based on a writer's firsthand observations and interviews. It is an engaging way to introduce field research. It asks students to rely neither on their memories nor on books they've read but on their abilities to attend to what they see and hear.

When students write profiles, they seek primarily to inform readers but also to engage their interest and entertain them. Just by singling out a place, person, or activity as a subject, a profile writer tells readers that it is important and worth their attention. Profiles are openly interpretive; they do not pretend to be objective reporting.

Writing a profile can be an unusually interesting project, since it takes students out into the community to meet new people and observe unfamiliar activities. Students practice observing, interviewing, notetaking, and writing activities basic to the work of investigative reporters; to naturalists, ecologists, geologists, anthropologists, sociologists, pollsters, and other academic researchers; and to doctors and psychologists. When students write up the results of their observations and interviews, they learn how to organize information gathered in firsthand research. This activity helps students develop their research and analytic skills.

All or most of the information in a profile comes from students' own observations. In the preceding chapter, students were asked to rely on their memories of events important in their personal lives. In this assignment, they must take notes at the time of the interview or observation or just after, so they are using a different kind of memory. This chapter also forms a bridge to the next chapter, in which students study and do another kind of explanatory writing, explaining concepts, which relies primarily on well-established information they've learned from books and articles, rather than on firsthand observations.

Since a profile may involve several trips off-campus, students should choose a subject as soon as possible. They will need help from you in scheduling their research. Advise them on the size and scope and on the amount of time you want them to spend on this project. A profile may be simple or complex, based on a single observation or interview (such as a sporting event, poetry reading, or boat show) or on several observational visits and interviews (such as to an emergency room, court of law, or local television studio).

The Guide to Writing in this chapter provides support for planning, researching, and writing a profile based on multiple observations and interviews; but it will also be very useful for students who do a smaller project. In addition, Chapter 12: Strategies for Field Research provides helpful advice on observing, interviewing, and writing up what is learned. You might want to have students read that chapter to discover how to plan and conduct observations and interviews.

Special Problems of This Writing Assignment

There are essentially two problems students have with this assignment. The first has to do with scheduling the research and the other with focusing the information.

To deal with the scheduling problem, the Guide to Writing recommends that students establish their own research schedules. But you might also set up deadlines for various stages of the project—such as deciding on a subject and arranging an interview or observation, writing up notes on observational visits and interviews, or writing the first draft—to help students keep on schedule. You could easily have students follow the guidelines for writing up their observations and interviews in Chapter 12: Strategies for Field Research and then use class time for peer workshops on these notes and write-ups.

Writing up notes and exchanging the write-ups with others in the class can also help students focus their profiles. The focusing problem results from the overwhelming quantity of information students usually gather. The more they work with their material—analyzing it, writing about it, finding connections and patterns in it—the more likely they are to develop an interpretation with which to organize the information.

Promising and Unpromising Topics

For many novice writers who have just arrived at a university (or a new city), the profile offers an ideal chance for exploration. Students should be encouraged to seek out unusual activities, people, or places. When you make the profile assignment, tell them to avoid topics with which they are overly familiar (for example, the summer job they have had for the last four years, their college dorm, etc.). If your students are writing a longer profile, they will need to pick a topic with plenty of activity, enough people for several interviews, and a place that can be described specifically (profiles about "the beach" or "downtown" generally don't work, for instance).

You should also be aware that this assignment may pose problems for some students. Those who do not have ready access to transportation may be encouraged to choose their subjects from the campus community. However, you should avoid limiting your students to campus choices, especially if you have a significant population of commuting students, who might instead be encouraged to focus their attention on subjects in their own neighborhoods. Extremely shy students pose a different kind of problem. Although this assignment does not lend itself well to collaborative writing, you might suggest that students conduct their observations together if they are focusing on the same place or activity. They could then work separately on the observation write-up.

Two other problems with selecting a profile topic are those of accessibility and security. Subjects that may sound exciting in theory may not be possible or appropriate in practice: A doctor or scientist may not be available for interviews; a military installation or a nuclear power plant may be off-limits to the general public.

Similarly, you should discourage students from exploring topics that are potentially dangerous. Students should think twice about profiling something like the county jail (which may be off-limits anyway), a neighborhood with a high incidence of crime, or some activity that presents a health or safety hazard. On the one hand, you don't want your students to select mundane or drab topics, but on the other hand, you should urge them to use discretion when picking a subject to profile.

You can spend class time exchanging topic choices, or you can circulate topic sheets. At the top of a sheet of paper, students write a tentative title for their profiles. Then they describe in two or three sentences the person, location, or activity that will be the subject of their profile. In one sentence they identify possible readers (class members, readers of a particular newspaper or magazine, or perhaps a special group of readers with a need to know what the writer will discover). These sheets then circulate around the class, with students writing questions or comments and even commenting on other students' comments.

We think it's a good idea for teachers to discuss and even approve students' topic choices, because students are unlikely to foresee the possibilities and problems of a topic.

CHAPTER INTRODUCTION

Writing in Your Other Courses

Writing in the Community

Writing in the Workplace

Profiles are common in academic and professional writing; for example, in education and anthropology courses, in journalism, in social work, and in business. With your students, you could analyze these assignments and writing situations, discuss how to gather information through observation and interviews, and determine how to interpret the information. You might also ask students to find other examples of this kind of writing by reviewing their textbooks, talking to instructors or employers, or looking through magazines or newspapers.

Practice Choosing a Profile Subject: A Collaborative Activity

This collaborative activity enables students to explore the rhetorical situation of the profile. The activity prepares them to approach the readings from the perspective of a writer, studying the ways that various writers have negotiated this rhetorical situation. It also prompts them to begin thinking about their own topics. As they try out an idea with two or three fellow students, they become aware of the important dimensions of purpose and audience.

Then they step back to examine the rhetorical situation of profiling a subject, and to think about the ways in which readers' expectations about and knowledge of the subject affect a writer's approach to it. Because students find this activity so engaging, you will need to remind them to shift from telling about their subjects to answering the questions in the text.

READINGS

The readings suggest a range of possibilities for profile writing. The anonymous author of "Soup" focuses on a person (Albert Yeganeh), while Cable focuses on a place (the Goodbody Mortuaries). Orenstein might be said to focus on a situation—that faced by teenage girls in the classroom. You might discuss the degree of objectivity the author of "Soup" brings to the essay and how that author uses interpreters (the customers) to make the subject comprehensible to the reader. Whereas Orenstein and Cable use narrative to organize their information, the author of "Soup" relies on the juxtaposition of different types of information.

Topics in Analysis Questions and Commentaries

These lists can serve as a valuable quick reference, enabling you in class or in conference to direct a student's attention to a particular feature in a question or commentary. The student may find ideas for addressing a particular problem in revising his or her draft. For example, if a student has difficulty with an opening, you might refer him or her to Cable's reading, particularly question 1 of Analyzing Writing Strategies.

The New Yorker, *"Soup"*	
Analyzing Writing Strategies	*Commentary: Focus and Informative Plan*
1. basic features	organization: topical
2. details	
Orenstein, *"The Daily Grind: Lessons in the Hidden Curriculum"*	
Analyzing Writing Strategies	*Commentary: Significance*
1. focus	comparison/contrast
2. time markers	specific narrative action
Cable, *"The Last Stop"*	
Analyzing Writing Strategies	*Commentary: Significance and Vivid Presentation*
1. opening strategies	significance
2. descriptions and dominant impression	vivid presentation

| **Soup** |
| The New Yorker |

"Soup" is a lively profile of an unusual takeout restaurant and its owner. We ask students to pay close attention to the use of dialogue in the essay. You might also ask students to imagine what kind of person would run a restaurant that serves only soup. What would they want to know about a person like this?

Connecting to Culture and Experience: Standards of Excellence

This activity, which might be handled in small groups or by the class as a whole, asks students to consider a central issue in the reading—dedication to quality on the job. Students may draw from their own experiences in school or at work to answer the questions, and they probably will have developed definite opinions about values in either environment. If you are asking your students to focus on the "identity and community" thematic strand, you might encourage them to address the issue of excellence in school. If you've chosen to focus on "work and career," you might ask them to limit their discussion to work experiences.

Analyzing Writing Strategies

1. This question asks students to measure "Soup" against the criteria for an effective profile. It encourages them to focus analytically on this particular essay and this genre. It also makes them conscious of the basic features of this kind of writing to prepare them to critique their own and others' profiles.

2. The restaurant is described as a tiny storefront in New York City, marked by an awning and an electric signboard. The key description of the interior occurs in paragraph 5, which details the cramped quarters, the case filled with fresh vegetables, and the prices of the soups, as well as a typical order for "any well-behaved customer." Students' impressions of the place will vary, but they will probably notice that it contributes to the portrait of Mr. Yeganeh, reflecting his single-minded drive.

Commentary: A Specific Focus and Informative Plan

Building on the first question in Analyzing Writing Strategies, the commentary looks at "Soup" to illustrate two of the basic features of profiles: a well-focused subject and an engaging and informative organization. We point out that although "Soup" focuses on Mr. Yeganeh, the writer includes abundant details about the place and the activity. You might use this opportunity to stress the importance of careful observation in addition to a thorough interview in gathering information for a profile. From the interview, the writer gleans Mr. Yeganeh's attitudes, ideas, and business methods. From observation, he picks up descriptive images and comments from customers that contribute to his vivid presentation of the Mr. Yeganeh working in his small restaurant.

The commentary also discusses a special type of organization—topical. Students may be surprised to realize that there is a most careful plan behind a profile like "Soup" that does not proceed chronologically. We explain in some detail how "Soup" is organized to help students see this topical structure. If they decide to profile a person or a place, it's likely they will use this method for organizing their essays.

The discussion following the scratch outline demonstrates the logic behind the organization of this profile, and it identifies and distinguishes between material derived from interviews and from observation. It further encourages students to think ahead to the process of writing a profile and choosing an appropriate plan for their own essays. You might ask students to come up with a chronological scratch outline for a profile of Yeganeh and to consider the relative advantages and disadvantages of each plan.

Considering Topics for Your Own Essay

Students will generate some very interesting or surprising possibilities in response to reading "Soup." Here again we help the students make the transition from reading to planning their own writing. Interesting or unusual people and places make promising profile topics for students (and readers). You might encourage students to return to this section—and similar sections in the following readings—when they begin the invention process.

The Daily Grind: Lessons in the Hidden Curriculum **Peggy Orenstein**	This selection by Peggy Orenstein profiles Amy Wilkinson and her experiences as an eighth-grader by focusing on her both before school starts for the day and later in her math class. This dual focus presents two sides of

Amy: an outgoing, confident leader and an inhibited, shy math student. Orenstein also profiles the interactions between the female teacher and her male and female students to depict the gender gap in American schools. You might ask students as they read to think about the larger social issues that contribute to this gender gap.

Connecting to Culture and Experience: Gender Equality

As usual, this section can be used in either a small-group or a large class setting, or in a combination of the two. You might also ask students to prepare for discussion by writing a journal entry. Since students will think back to their own experiences and observations, their responses may differ in interesting ways, especially if the class is made up of traditional and nontraditional, or older, students. This activity is particularly appropriate for students writing on the topic strand "identity and community."

Analyzing Writing Strategies

1. This question asks students to determine, through careful analysis, Orenstein's focus. Students may point to Amy's central position at the beginning of the profile as evidence that it focuses on a person. Others may note the attention that Orenstein pays to the interactions between the teacher and her students to support the view that she focuses on an activity. You might encourage students to think about Orenstein's purpose in writing the profile as they identify her focus.

2. Students might work through this activity in small groups or in pairs and then discuss their reflections on the effectiveness of the time markers as a class. At this point, you might guide the students to recognize when chronological organization is appropriate. Students seem to adopt this type of organization readily, either relying on the chronology of the interview or observation or on the chronology of the person's life to shape their essays. This question provides an opportunity to stress the importance of using temporal transitions to show the passage of time and provide cues for readers.

Commentary: Significance

This commentary focuses on showing as a strategy to convey significance, specifically on Orenstein's use of comparison and contrast. She contrasts Amy's behavior outside and inside the classroom, using specific narrative action, to create an impression of Amy. Orenstein also contrasts the aggression of the boys with the timidity of the girls, as well as the different reactions of the teacher to each, to emphasize the gender gap in the classroom. We point out that this strategy allows Orenstein to convey her interpretation without making it explicit. We also note, though, that she does make more direct comments that indicate her perspective. Students might compare the strategies for creating a dominant impression used by the writer of "Soup," who relies more on implication, with those of Orenstein, and then think about the writers' possible reasons for choosing these strategies.

Considering Topics for Your Own Essay

The suggestions for topics in this section will require students to think of people interacting, both physically and verbally. You might take this opportunity to discuss the importance of careful observation when profiling an activity—of watching actions and listening to conversations—in addition to interviewing the participants. You might assign this activity as a journal entry or refer students to it during the invention process.

> *The Last Stop*
> Brian Cable

Brian Cable profiles the Goodbody Mortuaries. His humorous tone is likely to please readers and encourage students to try humor in their own profiles. You might wish to discuss the difficulties inherent in controlling tone, especially humor.

Connecting to Culture and Experience: Death

The questions here point to an interesting aspect of American culture: our attitudes toward death. If students have faced death and attended funerals, these questions could lead to interesting discussions about different cultural traditions and attitudes concerning death. If Cable is correct, though, you may find students a bit reluctant to respond to these questions. That reluctance, of course, could present another topic for discussion. You might ask students to list, either as a whole class or in small groups, the various terms we use for death and dying and then explore the metaphors that lie behind the terms. What does it mean when we say someone "passed away," "croaked," was "iced," or was "wasted"?

Analyzing Writing Strategies

1. The opening quotation announces the topic of death and dying and, by mentioning the undertaker, even forecasts the specific focus of the profile. The attribution of the epigraph to Mark Twain may lead students to expect that the topic will receive a somewhat humorous treatment. Students will probably agree that whether the profile writers in this chapter begin their pieces with vivid images (Orenstein) or unusual or surprising quotations (Cable), the purpose is the same: to capture the reader's interest and suggest the topic of the profile. But we also want students to recognize that different subjects require different rhetorical strategies.

2. This question encourages students to make the connection between the specific details used to describe each room and the dominant impression Cable conveys. Students will probably note the contrast between the "homey, lived-in look" of the lobby and the "showroom" atmosphere of the casket room, with its bright lights highlighting the advantages of each coffin, especially the "'top of the line'" model. These rooms are contrasted with the chapel, with its "musty" smell and dim light. Students may note that the three rooms underscore the impression that the mortuary is above all a business dealing with the practical, physical aspects of death.

Commentary: Significance and Vivid Presentation

In this commentary we discuss the strategies that Cable uses to convey the significance of his subject, the Goodbody Mortuaries. We point out that he incorporates himself in his profile by using the first-person pronoun and directly expressing his views. He also makes his judgments clear in his descriptions and in the quotations he selects. Some students have been taught never to use first-person pronouns in formal or academic writing, but the commentary suggests that there are valid reasons for their use here. You might discuss this commentary in class to help clear up students' misconceptions about the use of the first-person point of view.

This commentary also discusses tone and the necessity of matching tone with subject matter. We emphasize that Cable's humor does not come at the expense of the mortuary workers, who are treated respectfully and presented objectively. You might point out that some of the humor comes directly from the quotations—from Cable's presenting, without comment, exactly what Deaver and Tim say.

Considering Topics for Your Own Essay

This task asks students to think about the role of preconceptions in profile writing. You might invite students to discuss their preconceptions of a variety of subjects as a way of helping them find subjects for their own profiles.

PURPOSE AND AUDIENCE

Remind students that awareness of purpose and audience should guide their work in developing a profile, in deciding what to include in the draft and revision, and in choosing how to organize the material. Whether they include visual details, dialogue, or metaphor; whether they organize narratively; whether they focus on a person or an activity; what dominant impression they convey—all these crucial decisions are influenced by what they want to achieve with particular readers.

BASIC FEATURES: PROFILES

In this section, we summarize our analysis of the reading selections, distilling four essential features of profile writing:

- A specific focus
- A vivid presentation
- An indication of the significance
- An engaging, informative plan

We illustrate our discussion of these features with extensive references to the readings.

GUIDE TO WRITING

We look through the pages of the Guide to Writing section of the chapter in class, commenting briefly on each section, to help students prepare for the work ahead.

Invention and Research

Here is a list of the invention activities:

- Finding a subject to write about
- Exploring your preconceptions

- Planning your project
- Posing some preliminary questions
- Reflecting on the significance
- Defining your purpose for your readers
- Formulating a tentative thesis statement
- Considering document design

The Invention and Research section guides students through a variety of activities designed to help them develop a large list of potential subjects, make thoughtful and informed choices, try out their choices with a sample audience, and generate a wealth of details that will be useful to them when they draft. We always give students an overview of the specific invention activities, making the significance of each one clear. The invention work for the profile is extensive. It includes not only the listing, collaborative, and exploring activities, but also activities to help students plan and execute the field research.

The first activity is Finding a Subject. Students are anxious to settle on a topic as soon as possible, ending the uncertainty they see as an obstacle to moving ahead. Some students will be convinced that they know exactly what they want to write about; others will look for a quick solution. However, there are good reasons why we ask students to list here as many possible subjects as they can. We often use a focused brainstorming session (as described earlier in this manual) to generate a large list on the board, to help students expand the range of their thinking about possible subjects. When students have a large list to choose from, they are less likely to settle on safe, predictable choices; they can feel more comfortable that they have made a good choice; and they will be less anxious if their first choice doesn't work out. We consider invention work so important in preparing students for drafting that we sometimes devote class time to reviewing it.

Exploring Your Preconceptions helps students see what they already know or think about the subject. Sometimes these preconceptions are later woven into the profile itself, as in Cable's piece; sometimes they help the writer frame the essay as a contrast to common perceptions of their subject. In any event, you might discuss with students the way our preconceptions about a subject determine not only our starting point, but also our approach, our selection of details, and even our ability to make sense of what we observe.

Planning Your Project is a useful guide for writers who are confused about how to start their research. It offers suggestions for planning and refers students to Chapter 12: Strategies for Field Research for additional guidance in observing and interviewing. Field research is quite challenging and interesting for students. Few have had any experience with it, but most students really enjoy it. We require students to revisit their subjects several times, to gather a rich array of details and impressions. They might focus on sensory details during their first visits, followed by interviews on the subsequent visits. Or they may interview several people on several different visits to get varying points of view.

In Posing Some Preliminary Questions we invite students to think carefully about the questions they will want to ask in their interviews. At this point in the invention process you might consider arranging for your whole class to conduct an interview with an interesting campus figure, such as a teaching assistant from another country or the director of a campus program. You might also take your class on a field trip, on- or off-campus, to observe a place or activity. Students may choose to do follow-up interviews or observations and write their profiles on these subjects, or they may choose other subjects. Either way, this activity will give students a model to follow in pursuing their own research.

In the next three invention sections we provide questions that direct students' attention to focus, purpose, and audience. Reflecting on the Significance helps them consider what they've learned about the subject and, through exploratory writing, discover a possible focus for their draft. In Defining Your Purpose for Your Readers we ask students to think specifically about their readers: who they are, what they know, and what the students want them to learn. We then suggest that students summarize what they've written in Reflecting on the Significance in the form of tentative thesis statements. We make it clear, however, that these sentences may not appear in this form in their essays and that instead they will more likely make such interpretations and evaluations implicitly rather than explicitly.

In the final section we encourage students to think about visual or audio materials that might accompany their profiles.

Testing Your Choice: A Collaborative Activity

Once students have a tentative subject in mind, the group inquiry will provide an opportunity to try it out on a sample audience of two or three students. The responses will help the writer see whether the subject is inherently interesting to a potential audience or whether interest will need to be created through an unexpected angle or an offbeat treatment. You might write some questions on the board to help students focus the discussion, for example:

- What is likely to be most interesting or surprising about your subject?
- How might you get the information you need to write about it?
- What made you choose this subject?
- What unusual twist or angle might you develop?

Planning and Drafting

If students have worked through the invention sequence thoughtfully and have revisited their subject several times, taking notes on each visit, they will be surprised at how much material they have collected. Sometimes students are overwhelmed by the task of turning this mountain of observations, impressions, and reflections into a coherent essay. The activities in this section are especially designed to help students absorb and analyze the material they have and set goals for organizing, outlining, and drafting the profile.

This is an excellent opportunity for a planning workshop, where students in small groups can try out alternatives for organizing their material; explore potential readers' interest in certain aspects of or details in the material collected; and experiment with possible ways of shaping the essay. Encourage them to have an open and wide-ranging discussion about their plan and questions for drafting.

If students find themselves struggling at this point, or if the material they've collected seems thin and unpromising, there are five suggestions you might make:

1. They might review the invention activities to see where they could be developed further.

2. They might revisit their subjects to gather more information.

3. They might do some library research to find background material on the subjects.

4. They might tell other students what they've learned about the subjects as a way to see how they might present them in drafts.

5. They might review the reading selections for ideas about organizing their own material.

Critical Reading Guide

We often set up an in-class workshop in which students work in pairs. You will want to allow extra time for this workshop, perhaps as much as fifty minutes or an hour, since drafts tend to be fairly long—often longer than the final essay will be. We encourage readers to write comments on the draft and on a separate sheet of paper so that writers will remember what they said. If you have made this a full-blown research project, you might schedule two or three workshops to review successive drafts, focusing perhaps on vividness of description first and organizational issues in later drafts.

Revising

Students need time to think about the critical comments from readers and to review drafts with some objectivity. The activities in this section will help them develop a plan for revising by rereading and outlining the draft, identifying problems in the draft, analyzing the features of the profile, focusing on readers' comments, and working to solve the problems. Students may work alone to complete these activities, but several of them can be productive for students working in small groups. For example, once students have a sense of the problems in the draft, they might work with two or three other students to develop solutions, using the problem-solving suggestions as a guide.

To help students make substantial rather than superficial revisions, we try to arrange a conference, and require them to complete the outline and problem-solving chart and bring it in with them. On this occasion, we often remind them that the chapter readings might now be maximally useful—as they return to them to consider the ways other writers have solved the problems they now face. After they've finished their essay, they'll have an opportunity in Reflecting on Your Writing to think about how they solved problems in their drafts.

Editing and Proofreading

At this point, students will proofread to polish their final drafts, correcting errors of mechanics, usage, punctuation, and spelling. You might ask students to edit outside of class, or in class with your guidance. You might also put students in pairs and ask them to proofread each other's essays.

REFLECTING ON YOUR WRITING

Like the previous chapter, this chapter concludes by asking students to reflect carefully on their experiences with the type of writing introduced in the chapter. Students are asked to reexamine the process of writing their own profiles and to explain how they solved a particular problem.

RESPONDING TO PROFILES

Problems like the ones listed below are typical of students' writing of profiles:

Subject

- The essay simply reports information and does not reveal a point of view or an angle on the subject.
- The angle is too pat and predictable, and offers nothing new about the subject: "Hell's Angels are actually just ordinary folks like you and me, with families, picnics, and so on."
- The treatment of the subject is superficial; the essay reads like an advertisement for the place or person.

Presentation

- The essay tells rather than shows what happened at the site or in an interview.
- The organization is problematic: Narrative structure breaks down, topical structure is unpredictable, or organization is lacking altogether.

- Too much of the essay is concerned with the writer's process: "I cautiously turned the glistening knob of the main door, approached the receptionist, and blurted out, 'I am writing an assignment. I had an appointment to speak with Ms. Simpson.'"
- There is a wealth of information but no effective organization of it, or conversely, there is too little detail.
- The essay lacks continuity; it seems as though the write-ups have simply been "stapled" together.

Pace

- Too much irrelevant information in some places slows down the pace.
- The narrative rushes over places where the reader would like more information.
- The pace is uneven or does not build tension or interest as a narrative.
- The pace is slowed down by the unnecessary description of the writer's activities: "We were late because we stopped for lunch before we met Mr. Sanchez, and the service in the restaurant was very slow."

PREPARING FOR CONFERENCES

If you hold conferences with your students on their drafts, you could have them prepare for the conference by filling in the form on the following page.

CHAPTER 4: EXPLAINING A CONCEPT

THE WRITING ASSIGNMENT

Write an essay about a concept that interests you and that you want to study further. When you have a good understanding of the concept, explain it to your readers, considering carefully what they already know about it and how your essay might add to what they know.

The Nature of the Writing Assignment

This assignment gives students practice in the most common kind of writing they are likely to encounter: writing to convey helpful and interesting information. We like to give students a fairly free rein in choosing their concepts. We urge them to be guided by their academic or extracurricular interests, but we require that their subjects be significant and their information new and interesting for a number of readers.

Aside from requiring fresh, interesting information, this assignment's main demand of a writer is clarity. Reporting information is an exercise in organization, in marshaling available information into a pattern that will be easy for readers to see. The summary of Basic Features reviews for students a

PREPARING FOR A CONFERENCE: CHAPTER 3

Before the conference, write answers to the questions below. Bring your invention writing and first draft to the conference.

1. What subject are you profiling? Why did you choose it? What is the single most surprising thing you've learned about it?

2. Who are your readers? How did your awareness of them influence the way you wrote this draft? Be specific.

3. Explain briefly the plan of your essay—your beginning, ending, and sequencing of observations and comments. Why is this plan especially appropriate for your readers? Note one or two ways to improve your plan.

4. What is your interpretation? How did you discover it, and how has it helped you to focus and unify your draft?

5. If you were to return for one more visit, what would you like to find out? Whom would you try to talk to? What information do you still need about the subject?

6. What are you most pleased with in this draft? Be specific.

7. What specifically do you need to do next to revise your draft? List any problems you see in the draft as well as any that have been pointed out by other readers. Say briefly how you might attempt to solve these problems. Use the back of this form for these notes. (If you have completed the text's Revising plan, bring it with you to the conference instead of answering this question.)

set of strategies including definition, classification, process narration, comparison and contrast, and cause and effect. The assignment invites the student writer to use these strategies in a combination that suits the subject, the readers, and the writer's point.

The essay that explains a concept may be used to introduce students to techniques of library research and to styles of documenting sources (Chapter 14: Strategies for Using and Acknowledging Sources), and it can become an extended term paper. This chapter introduces students to strategies that they will need again when they write arguments in subsequent chapters, as well as for essay exams or reports for classes. As they gain control of these writing strategies, students learn new ways to organize information, to phrase it in their own words, and thus to make it their own. The strategies are the basic tools with which they can make writing a way of learning, of assimilating new knowledge.

If your students are going from Chapter 3 to Chapter 4, you might want to point out some of the similarities and differences between observational and explanatory writing. Both aim to present information in a way that readers will find intelligible and interesting. Observational writing is derived mainly from the writer's firsthand experiences and observation, and it often relies on narrative and vivid description to communicate what the writer has seen or learned about the subject. Explanatory writing, on the other hand, is typically derived from a variety of sources that may include the writer's personal experience and observation, but it usually depends heavily on what the writer has learned from others through reading and listening. Writers of explanation analyze and synthesize, interpret and summarize the work of others. They present information, draw connections, and discuss implications.

In this chapter, we focus on a particular aim of explanatory writing— writing to explain concepts. This focus enables students to work on the kind of explanation they are reading and writing in most of their courses. Throughout the disciplines, particularly in introductory courses, students are learning basic concepts. They learn by reading and by writing. Understanding the rhetoric of explanatory discourse can help them become better learners as well as more effective explainers.

Special Problems of This Writing Assignment

In our experience, the main problems that student writers have with this assignment fall into two categories: choosing an appropriate concept and then analyzing and synthesizing the available information on it. One solution to the problem of topic choice is to encourage students to write about subjects introduced in their other courses. In the section Invention and Research, some academic subjects are suggested. This assignment lends itself well to cross-disciplinary writing. We also suggest possible concepts associated with the thematic strands "identity and community" or "work and career." If you are not limiting your students to one of the thematic strands, and if students lack confidence in writing about academic subjects, you might allow them to write about concepts drawn from their extracurricular interests.

Students may ask you "What *is* a concept?" We propose an answer which paraphrases the dictionary definition: *a general idea derived from specific instances.* Each reading in this chapter enables students to understand that concepts are formed from many specific observations or instances. It is also interesting to consider that certain concepts can be intuited or fully recognized long before they are named.

Students will need your help in finding a focus for their essays. Most concepts are too big — too much is known about them — for a college essay, even a long research paper. Consequently, you may want students to write about only one *aspect* of the concept. The readings are useful in illustrating how one narrows a concept to a specific aspect and focus. For example, Toufexis explains the concept of love narrowed to a specific aspect, sexual love. She focuses even more narrowly on the chemistry of love. You might encourage students to see their own search for a topic as a process of moving from a large concept to a specific aspect with a specific focus. Notice how the invention activities are set up to lead students first to a broad overview of the concept and then to a focus on one interesting aspect of it. Only with a focus in mind do they begin collecting research information.

When we teach this assignment, we discuss with students their concept choice and the concept focus. We involve the whole class in assessing each other's topic choices and foci.

Presenting a technical concept in a way that is clear and interesting to a general audience challenges student writers. Students may become very concerned with the specificity and accuracy of the information they report and, in the process, forget about engaging readers' interest. The purpose of the essay is to give readers interesting new knowledge. The greatest challenge of this assignment may not be the analysis and selection of information, but the presenting of information in a way that allows readers to understand key terms, follow the organization of the essay, and remain interested in the topic. To succeed with this challenge, students will need to pay particular attention to the tone they use, the cues they provide for readers (see Chapter 8), and the defining and classifying strategies they use.

The assignment can also be a good way to introduce students to library research. The student who knows little about a concept but is curious about it can gather information from the library or by talking with experts. You may want to require some library research from all students, referring them to Chapter 13: Strategies for Library and Internet Research and Chapter 14: Strategies for Using and Acknowledging Sources.

The most important problem students have with this writing task is that they may allow themselves to be eclipsed by their sources. Their essays then become dumping grounds for unprocessed information, leaving readers to guess at its significance. One of the hardest things for student writers to do is to discover what they want readers to learn about the information. Without this particular purpose, the essay will be a pointless collection of facts, drifting like an abandoned ship. An essay explaining concepts needs to be organized around a main point or thesis.

Related to discovering an informative purpose is the problem of selecting and arranging the information, using the range of available strategies to achieve the purpose. Student writers often have difficulty designing a plan that will organize the information in a way that readers will find interesting and comprehensible. A common problem is that an essay grasps at a simple, ready-made structure, often following the writer's process of discovering the information and ignoring what readers know or need to know about the subject. Again, analyzing the structure of the readings can show students how to avoid this problem. Further advice on essay structure can be found in Chapter 8: Strategies for Cueing Readers.

Promising and Unpromising Topics

The least problematic topics are those that are established concepts, such as existentialism or bilingualism. Students who choose such topics will probably have little difficulty finding and maintaining a conceptual focus. Other kinds of topics are no less promising, but they can be problematic in different ways:

- *Concepts undergoing change:* Some concepts may be treated from a static and historical perspective. For example, the concept of musical harmony can be considered to be stable and fixed. It might appear this way if one researched it only through reference sources and books. On the other hand, if one researched extensively in specialized periodicals, one could discover challenges by avant-garde musicians to traditional concepts of harmony. In this case, either treatment seems justified, depending on the purpose and audience. For certain other concepts, however, acknowledgment of recent developments and rapidly evolving trends seems vital to an accurate portrayal of the concept; notions of mental illness and democracy, for example, have undergone major transformations in recent years.

- *Concepts about controversial issues:* If your course will cover both explanatory writing (Chapter 4) and persuasive writing (Chapters 5–7), now is the time to begin discussing with your students the differences between the two genres. For this essay, we emphasize that their opinions should not be foregrounded or obviously stated, though they will certainly guide students' selection and presentation of material. Those who have chosen a concept they have strong feelings about, e.g., racism or recycling, will need your guidance to help them shape a balanced, informative treatment of the topic, rather than a partisan, argumentative one. Suggest that students save the argumentative approach for the next assignment, the position paper.

- *Concepts about personal life:* Some students may be attracted to concepts for which personal experience will be their sole resource. Topics in this category from the Collaborative Activity section include friendship, success, and maturity. Students may be more likely to choose these topics if the class has already done personal experience writing (Chapters 2–3). While this focus is certainly valid, you may want to encourage students to move beyond personal experience to published sources. Your guidance here can be supportive and enlightening: Many students will be surprised to discover that library sources are available on such concepts as friendship and maturity, and that material from these sources may be interwoven with personal anecdotes to create an effective essay.

CHAPTER INTRODUCTION

Writing in Your Other Courses

Writing in the Community

Writing in the Workplace

These examples of explaining concepts come from college courses, from community programs, and from the workplace. Working through this chapter and writing their own essays on a concept will familiarize students with the central role concept definition and explanation play in all fields of inquiry inside the academy and in the real world.

Practice Explaining a Concept: A Collaborative Activity

This activity gives students their first classroom opportunity to explain a concept—in this case orally, briefly, and informally—to a small group of their peers. This activity shouldn't take more than fifteen minutes. If the list of possible concepts does not allow sufficient choice, you could lead a class brainstorming session to come up with other possible concepts. Before they begin the activity, you could review with students the interactive nature of the exercise: Following the mini-presentations, listeners ask questions that elicit additional information necessary to clarify the concept. The questions at the end of the activity help students recognize the importance of audience in shaping their explanations.

READINGS

Topics in Analysis Questions and Commentaries

For your convenience, we list below all the discourse topics addressed in each of the Analyzing Writing Strategies and Commentary sections. This list can serve as a quick reference in class or in conference to direct a student's attention to a question or commentary which addresses an area the student needs to work on in revising his or her draft. For example, if a student's draft would benefit from more examples, you could suggest reviewing Ngo from the perspective of question 2 and the commentary.

Toufexis, "Love: The Right Chemistry"	
Analyzing Writing Strategies	Commentary: A Focused Concept and Careful Use of Sources
1. features of concept explanations	using sources
2. classifying	focus cueing the reader
Potera, "Internet Addiction"	
Analyzing Writing Strategies	Commentary: Defining an Emerging Phenomenon
1. using sources	definition
2. cause and effect	
Ngo, "Cannibalism: It Still Exists"	
Analyzing Writing Strategies	Commentary: A Logical Plan
1. classification	classifying
2. examples	organization

> Love: The Right Chemistry
> Anastasia Toufexis

Students usually find this to be an informative and entertaining essay: It shows that explanatory writing need not be dry or dull. Toufexis comes across as an expert on her subject, but she is not a professional scientist. Her authority, like that of students as they write their own essays, comes from research into secondary sources.

Connecting to Culture and Experience: Love Maps

This section, which is particularly useful for students focusing on the thematic strand "identity and community," asks students to respond to Toufexis's essay first on a personal level and then to consider the cultural dimensions of sexual attraction. This section could be assigned initially as a written journal entry; in-class follow-up could include whole-class or small-group discussion.

Analyzing Writing Strategies

1. This question asks students to examine Toufexis's essay in light of what we've said about the aims and characteristics of concept explanations. By looking closely at Toufexis's essay both for what is and is not there, students can get a better understanding of what this kind of writing tries to accomplish.

2. Here is a possible scratch outline of paragraphs 9–15:

- Love as a chemical reaction (9)
- The chemical reactions to falling in love: amphetamines (10)
- The body builds up tolerance to these chemicals (11–12)
- The chemical reactions to long-term romances: endorphins (13)
- Comparison of the two types of chemical reactions (14)
- Another chemical reaction to love: oxytocin (15)

Students will note that Toufexis divides and orders her information about the chemistry of love according to the familiar stages of romance. They may have differing views about her success; the point of this exercise is that the students support their views with careful analysis.

Commentary: A Focused Concept and Careful Use of Sources

This commentary helps students concentrate on three fundamental elements of concept explanation: focusing on a specific aspect, using sources, and cueing the reader. Students will likely be drawn to large concepts, so you probably cannot stress too much the importance of focusing narrowly on a specific aspect. Toufexis's essay offers an opportunity to demonstrate how a writer chooses a focus.

The commentary also discusses Toufexis's use of sources, pointing out that she makes use of both printed sources and interviews in gathering information for her essay. While most students will rely primarily on printed sources in gathering material for their own essays, you might refer those who will use interviews as well to Chapter 12: Strategies for Field Research for valuable advice on interviewing. You may also want to remind students that they will need to document their sources considerably more thoroughly than Toufexis needs to. This point can bear quite a bit of emphasis, as few students have extensive experience with the thorough and formal citation of sources demanded in academic writing. Chapter 13: Strategies for Library and Internet Research and Chapter 14: Strategies for Using and Acknowledging Sources will be particularly valuable resources for this assignment.

While students have already examined Toufexis's use of transitions in the second question for analysis, the commentary points out other types of cues and refers students to Chapter 8: Strategies for Cueing Readers for a more detailed discussion of these important devices.

Considering Topics for Your Own Essay

This activity could function as a pre-invention exercise, perhaps for a journal entry. Though you need not present it to students as a way of generating possible topics for their own essays (indeed, to do so might inhibit their listing), you might ask them to refer back to these lists during invention.

This section offers rich possibilities for writing in an area that will be of interest to many students. The subject of love or romance also lends itself to a pleasing complementariness of printed sources and personal anecdotes.

> **Internet Addiction**
> Carol Potera

Students who have grown up with personal computers and the Internet may find this essay engaging and may have strong views about the concept of Internet addiction. In the introduction to this reading we ask students to think about their own time on the Internet: about how much of it is devoted to academic or work-related use and how much is devoted to diversion.

Connecting to Culture and Experience: Wasting Time Online

The questions in this section will lead to interesting discussion, either in small groups or as a class—even perhaps in an online discussion. You might first have students write their answers and then share them with others.

Analyzing Writing Strategies

1. These questions focus students' attention on Potera's sources and ask them to take particular note of the qualifications that give authority to her experts. Evaluating Potera's sources will alert students to the necessity of evaluating their own possible sources and carefully choosing the ones they use.

2. These questions ask students to analyze Potera's presentation of causes and effects. They will recognize that research findings are important in explanatory writing, and they will be familiar with the use of anecdotes if they have written essays for one or both of the previous chapters (Chapter 2: Remembering Events and Chapter 3: Writing Profiles), but they might not recognize the role anecdotes can play in essays explaining concepts.

Commentary: Defining an Emerging Phenomenon

Students will of course need to define their concepts and other terms in the essays they write for this assignment. In this commentary we focus on the particular demands of defining relatively new concepts for which there are no established definitions. We point out that Potera presents the debate over what to call the behavior she explores without taking sides in the debate and that she finally uses the term preferred by one expert. She then uses anecdotes as well as scientific findings for her definition of the term *Internet addiction,* which extends over several paragraphs. This commentary provides an opportunity to introduce students to the extended definition as a strategy that they might also incorporate into their own essays. You might also use this commentary to reinforce the distinction between writing to explain and writing to support a position.

Considering Topics for Your Own Essay

The topics listed here are ones that students might be able to explore in their psychology or sociology classes. In addition to these sources, you might suggest that students gather information by interviewing their instructors in these classes or by obtaining information through the campus health or wellness center. You might refer students to this section when they are making their lists during invention, especially if they are following the "identity and community" topic strand.

Cannibalism: It Still Exists Linh Kieu Ngo	This essay, written when the author was a first-year college student, effectively explains a disturbing but intriguing concept. Students will find the many examples absorbing and will likely recognize the value of this strategy for their own writing.

Connecting to Culture and Experience: Taboos

The questions in this section will no doubt stimulate lively debate. To allow all students to discuss the issues, you might assign this section as a small-group activity or as a topic for an online discussion. A whole-class discussion would be particularly helpful for exploring the cultural origins of the taboo against cannibalism.

Analyzing Writing Strategies

1. As we have done in the commentaries for Potera's essay and for "The New Terrorism," we again focus on definition in this analysis question. In this case we begin by pointing out that Ngo classifies cannibalism before offering definitions of its five types. Students might notice that in addition to the examples that illustrate, he contrasts the five types to clarify the definitions.

2. This question asks students to make a careful analysis of one example and to judge its effectiveness. You might have students work in small groups, each with a different example, and then share their findings with the class. You might then encourage them to compare the examples to determine which illustrate the concept more effectively.

Commentary: A Logical Plan

In this commentary we focus on Ngo's choice of classification as an ordering principle to explain the concept of cannibalism. We also point out that the explanation moves logically from most to least familiar, and from least to most complex. Students will recognize that the plan of this essay works well in part because Ngo effectively uses cues like forecasting and transitional sentences to ease his readers' way. You might send students back to this commentary when they are planning their own essays. You could also ask them to compare the plan of Ngo's essay with that of Toufexis's essay, which also relies on classification.

Considering Topics for Your Own Essay

This list of topics should elicit strong reactions, which may be profitably channeled into interesting writing. You could take this opportunity to explore possible sources for material on these subjects. For example, students might look to their courses in sociology, anthropology, or psychology for information and consider consulting their instructors as experts. You might also ask students to return to this section when they begin the invention activities for this chapter.

PURPOSE AND AUDIENCE

This section highlights the goals of explanatory writing and stresses that writers must take on the role of expert to engage and inform readers.

BASIC FEATURES: EXPLAINING CONCEPTS

Here is a list of the features covered in this section. It is useful to have students read this section once before they begin work on invention and then to reread it as they are making their revision plans.

- A focused concept
- An appeal to readers' interests
- A logical plan
- Clear definitions
- Appropriate writing strategies
- Careful use of sources

GUIDE TO WRITING

Invention and Research

Here is a list of the invention activities:

- Finding a concept to write about
- Researching the concept
- Focusing the concept
- Testing your choice
- Considering explanatory strategies
- Considering document design
- Defining your purpose for your readers
- Formulating a tentative thesis statement

It will be a good idea to familiarize your students with these steps before they actually begin the invention process. Suggest that they begin work right away but spread the work out over several sessions. You can help them stay on track by requiring that they reach a certain point by a certain class meeting.

Testing Your Choice: A Collaborative Activity

At the Testing Your Choice stage of invention, we invite students to meet in small groups to try out their ideas on each other.

Planning and Drafting

The purpose of this section is to help students move smoothly from invention to drafting. After students take time to review their invention writings, they should set some goals for their essays. If there is time, students could explain their goals to you in a brief conference, or they could explain them to one another in small groups.

Critical Reading Guide

We usually urge students to write out comments and suggestions. Students who have participated in peer review of drafts in the past may have made only marginal comments on the draft itself, and may have exchanged oral comments with another student. Comments in writing help later when the writer is trying to make a revising plan.

Revising

Working with this section will enable your students to decide what changes they want to make and to carry out these revisions effectively. During this phase of the writing process you might remind them that they can review the summary of Basic Features, look at how the writers in this chapter solved similar problems, study the critical comments they received from their peers, or discuss their plans for revisions with you.

Students who seriously question their drafts in light of the guidelines in this section will probably revise their essays substantially. You could point out to students how recursive the process is; as we move from examining readings to doing invention to getting critical comments to making our revision plans, we lead ourselves back through the possibilities for developing an essay of this type, though the tasks are posed differently now.

We find it useful to emphasize to students the importance of rereading and considering the draft *as a whole* before contemplating specific revision changes. Some students resist this step; once they have secured feedback from their classmates, they want to proceed directly to revising their drafts.

You might ask students to make or at least begin their plan for revision under your guidance. If they are able to study their peers' comments, reread their drafts carefully, and compose a scratch outline while they are in the classroom with you available as a resource, they will be well launched into the process and be able to revise their drafts on their own. Alternatively, students could review their plans at the next class meeting to ensure that they're on track. Then you could select and duplicate the best revision plan and ask the writer to present it to the class as a model.

Editing and Proofreading

At this point, we suggest that students read through their essays at least three times to check for errors in paragraphs, sentences, and words. You might ask students to edit outside of class, or in class with your guidance. You might also put students in pairs and ask them to proofread each other's essays.

REFLECTING ON YOUR WRITING

Once students have completed their own essays, we ask them to reflect carefully on their experiences with writing concept explanations. Students are asked to reexamine the process of writing their own essays and to explain how they solved a particular problem.

RESPONDING TO ESSAYS EXPLAINING CONCEPTS

Here are some typical problems you might find with students' concept explanations:

Concept

- The essay is unfocused. It is not clear what point the writer is trying to make about this concept.
- The writer apparently has not mastered the concept—relies too much on sources and jargon, lacks authority.
- The explanation seems inappropriate for the audience—telling them too much or too little.

Plan

- The essay is hard to follow.
- The writer neglects to forecast the plan and provide transitions.
- The information needs to be rearranged to make more sense.

Definitions and Other Writing Strategies

- Definitions of terms likely to be unfamiliar to readers are inadequate.
- The writer has not made use of clearly relevant strategies of presenting information—for example, comparison and contrast, classification, and cause and effect.

- Examples don't seem to have a clear purpose or point.
- The writer concentrates on recent developments, when readers need background or historical information.
- Instead of reporting on a concept, the writer takes a position on an issue related to the concept.

Sources

- The citations and sources reveal a superficial or incomplete search for information.
- Certain sources are inappropriate, dated, or peripheral.
- The essay relies too much or too little on quoted material.
- Quoted material is not integrated smoothly into the writer's text.
- Sources cited are not in the reference list.
- Citations and references do not consistently follow an accepted documentation style.

PREPARING FOR CONFERENCES

If you hold conferences with your students on their drafts, you could have them prepare for the conference by filling in the form on the following page.

CHAPTER 5: ARGUING A POSITION

THE WRITING ASSIGNMENT

Write an essay on a controversial issue. Learn more about the issue and take a position on it. Present the issue to readers, and develop an argument for the purpose of confirming, challenging, or changing your readers' views on the issue.

The Nature of the Writing Assignment

With this assignment, students begin the third and perhaps most challenging kind of writing featured in this book—argumentation. The sequence of three types of argumentative writing includes the position paper (Chapter 5), proposal (Chapter 6), and evaluation (Chapter 7). Whether you teach all or a selection of these chapters, Chapter 5 along with Chapter 11: Strategies for Arguing will serve as an excellent introduction to the basic rhetorical concepts and strategies of argumentative writing.

As the first chapter in the sequence, Chapter 5 introduces the idea of developing an argumentative strategy that reflects the writer's purpose given

PREPARING FOR A CONFERENCE: CHAPTER 4

Before the conference, write answers to the questions below. Bring your invention writing and first draft to the conference.

1. What concept are you explaining? How did you come to choose it?

2. Who are your readers? What do you assume they already know about your concept? How did these assumptions influence how you decided to focus your explanation?

3. What main point do you make about your concept?

4. Explain briefly what writing strategies you decided to use — defining, classifying, comparing and contrasting, examining cause and effect, narrating a process — and why they seem appropriate.

5. Describe your organizational plan. How does the essay begin and end? How is the body of information presented?

6. What are you most pleased with in this draft? Be specific.

7. What specifically do you need to do next to revise your draft? List any problems you see in the draft or any that have been pointed out by other readers. Say briefly how you might attempt to solve these problems. Use the back of this form for these notes. (If you have completed the text's Revising plan, bring it with you to the conference instead of answering this question.)

the particular audience being addressed. This strategy informs the whole range of writing decisions from choosing an issue to anticipating opposing arguments to establishing a credible tone. Chapter 5 shows the full rhetorical context for such decisions. It is linked through a system of cross-references to the argumentative strategies in Chapter 11: Strategies for Arguing, where making claims, presenting evidence, refuting opposing arguments, and avoiding logical fallacies are discussed and illustrated in detail.

When students take a position on a controversial issue, they discover not only that people differ in their opinions, but also that they have good reasons for their different views. They learn to respect the complexity of these issues and the subtlety of others' reasoning. Because these chapters emphasize the rhetorical aspects of argumentation, they help students avoid polemics.

The writing assignment requires students to examine the issue critically. Instead of framing an argument to support an already formed opinion, we encourage students to analyze and evaluate the pros and cons of the issue before reaching their own conclusions. We urge them to examine their own underlying assumptions as critically as they would those of their opponents. We want them to recognize the value of thinking through the issue and of basing their position on solid reasoning and evidence, not merely to convince others but for their own sakes as well.

Special Problems of This Writing Assignment

Probably the greatest problem students encounter when they begin writing position papers is mistaking assertion for argumentation. This problem manifests itself in sweeping generalizations unsupported by reasons and evidence. Students with little experience developing an argument usually assume that all they need do is state what they think. They don't realize that they have to give the reasons for their position or offer evidence to support it. Nor do they recognize how important it is to anticipate readers' opposing arguments and to either modify their own position by acknowledging good points or defend it by refuting arguments with which they disagree.

For some students, the essential problem is lack of experience in setting out their reasons in a way that others can follow. For them, reading a diversity of arguments will provide instructive illustrations. If, however, the problem stems from the habit of relying on unexamined assumptions and biases, then the solution becomes more difficult. These students need first to accept the value of introspection and reasoning. They must recognize that the aim of argumentation is not merely to voice your own opinion but to examine it critically.

The root of the problem might be cognitive as well as emotional immaturity. Students who have not yet overcome their own egotism have little experience with other points of view; therefore, they have few strategies for self-analysis, let alone for audience analysis. They may be able to assert their own opinions forcefully but tend to have difficulty looking critically at their own assumptions or presenting a train of thought to others. In our experience, students with this kind of problem respond well when argumentative writing is presented as an act of communication rather than as an act of aggression. When the emphasis is on creating common ground instead of squashing your opponents into the ground, students feel less defensive and more open to alternative ways of seeing.

Promising and Unpromising Topics

We have found that there is no simple rule for prejudging the promise of topics for position papers. Many experienced instructors feel differently. For example, they often eliminate from consideration issues having to do with matters of faith like abortion and creationism. We find, however, that students can often handle issues such as these if they take other points of view seriously. What we find most limiting is lack of information. If students are not well informed about a topic and do not have the time or inclination to inform themselves, then their argument is likely to be fatuous—full of generalizations and lacking in reasons and evidence.

Without making the assignment a full-blown research project, you might encourage students to discuss the issue with others and to do some reading about it. Exploring opposing views should be a routine part of the invention process. Sometimes, however, students make their research one-sided. It is good to seek reasons and evidence to support a position, but students also need to learn about the other side. They need to be able to anticipate opposing arguments and to recognize values and concerns they may share with others.

In the Guide to Writing we offer a list of possibilities to get students thinking about issues they could write about. Many of the topics we suggest are ones we think students will know and also care about. Caring about the topic is essential for good writing, particularly for argumentative writing. This requirement comes as a surprise to some students and may even be threatening to them. We have been amazed at how many students are reluctant to express an opinion. Sometimes there is a cultural basis to their resistance. They may have been taught that it is inappropriate for them to argue assertively. Some have been made to feel that they know too little to have an opinion worth sharing. Others believe that they are in college to consume ideas and opinions, not to produce them. For these students, we emphasize the process over the product. We explain that taking a position teaches them to analyze issues critically and to evaluate arguments pro and con. With experience, students gain confidence in their reasoning abilities and come to enjoy developing a thoughtful, well-supported argument.

CHAPTER INTRODUCTION

Writing in Your Other Courses

Writing in the Community

Writing in the Workplace

Reading and writing about controversial issues is common in all areas of one's life, as the examples included here suggest. As a journal assignment, you might ask students to find similar examples from their other courses, from newspaper op-ed pages, from professional journals, or from their own workplaces and describe them as a journal entry. An in-class discussion of these entries will stress the significance of this genre.

Practice Arguing a Position: A Collaborative Activity

This activity gives students a preview of the process of writing a position paper. The most important part of the activity is the reflection at the end. Students are likely to discover that researching their topics will be essential to making a convincing argument. You might ask students from each group to speak to the class for a few minutes about their experiences.

Readings

These three readings should be interesting and challenging to students. One treats a controversial issue of public policy. The next essays deal with sports: the first, with the funding of women's college sports, and the other, written by a first-year college student, with children's participation in competitive sports. All are on important, controversial topics. From these examples, students can see how position papers deal with fundamental ethical questions.

Topics in Analysis Questions and Commentaries

These lists can serve as a quick reference to help you plan your discussion of discourse features either in class or in conferences.

Why Shouldn't Society Treat Substance Abusers?   Alan I. Leshner

In this essay, which was originally published as a newspaper column, Leshner argues that the treatment of individuals addicted to drugs is good public policy. In this introduction, we highlight the position of authority from which he addresses this issue and note that although he uses scientific research to support his view, he follows the specific conventions of the journalistic medium in dealing with sources.

Connecting to Culture and Experience: Addiction

This activity, designed for small groups, asks students to build a definition of *addiction* based on their own experiences and on cultural perceptions. The notion that addictions may sometimes be beneficial might be new to stu-

Leshner, "Why Shouldn't Society Treat Substance Abusers"	
Analyzing Writing Strategies 1. features of position papers 2. anticipating objections and questions	*Commentary: Convincing Support* examples authorities and statistics
Nelson, "Adventures in Equality"	
Analyzing Writing Strategies 1. presenting the issue 2. support	*Commentary: Anticipating Opposing Positions* acknowledging other positions conceding valid points refuting other positions
Statsky, "Children Need to Play, Not Compete"	
Analyzing Writing Strategies 1. anecdotes 2. citing sources 3. examples	*Commentary: A Clear Position* qualifying the position forecasting

dents. Asking them to examine their own assumptions and those of their culture will lead to interesting discussions, which will be particularly useful to students who are working with the "identity and community" topic strand.

Analyzing Writing Strategies

1. As we always do with the first analysis question of the first reading, we ask students to measure Leshner's essay against the criteria for this genre. This question will increase students' awareness of the basic features of position papers as they read the other essays in the text, other students' essays, and their own.

2. Before students respond to this question, you might discuss Leshner's audience with them. Analyzing Leshner's refutation of readers' objections will help prepare students to deal with objections to their own positions.

Commentary: Convincing Support

This commentary focuses on Leshner's use of examples, statistics, and authorities to support his position. We note, as we did in the introduction, that he follows conventions for giving credit to his sources that are different from those the students will be expected to follow in their own essays. Even though he does not cite specific sources for his statistics, he backs them up using the authority of the research institutions, his own authority, and the authority of science. Students may take from this commentary techniques for analyzing the use of authority in essays they read and write. You might return to this section when you discuss Nelson's and Statsky's citation styles and when students begin to document their own sources.

See the following exercise based on this reading in Chapter 11: Strategies for Arguing:

- Exercise 11.5 on using statistics

Considering Topics for Your Own Essay

This section suggests other topics dealing with public policy issues. You might assign it as a journal entry, as a small-group activity, or as a whole-class brainstorming session.

> *Adventures*
> *in Equality*
> **Mariah Burton Nelson**

Students will find the issue addressed in this essay compelling and will likely have strong opinions about Nelson's position. In our introduction, we provide information about the original publication of this excerpt and ask students to look at Nelson's challenge to men. You might discuss Nelson's audience with students before they begin the essay.

Connecting to Culture and Experience: Equity

This section asks students to examine their own values concerning the issue of gender equity in college sports. You might prepare students for this activity by discussing the meaning of the word *equity* and then ask students to list, perhaps in their journals, the values connected to college sports that they see as important. Then they can address the questions in this section in small groups.

Analyzing Writing Strategies

1. This question focuses on the way in which Nelson presents her issue. First, as we point out, she gives a history of the suits filed by women athletes and coaches to push the enforcement of the 1972 law. Then she identifies the reasons for the suits and provides statistics to support her contention that football is responsible for the inequities. You might return to this analysis section when students are working out ways to present their own issues.

2. This analysis activity helps students see how writers use quotations to support their own positions and to acknowledge opposing positions. Students might work together in small groups or in pairs to analyze Nelson's use of sources.

Commentary: Anticipating Opposing Positions

To reinforce our previous directions concerning counterarguments, we focus in this commentary on Nelson's strategies for dealing with opposing positions. We advise students that a writer's readers and purpose will determine how they choose to counterargue. Students may be surprised to discover that Nelson devotes half of her essay to refuting the reasons for the opposing view. We also discuss the rhetorical advantage of repeating the same phrase to introduce the points that she refutes. Since students frequently tend to overlook the need to consider opposing views in their attempts to establish their own positions, you might want to devote class time to going over this commentary.

Considering Topics for Your Own Essay

This section encourages students to consider local campus or community issues for their own essays. The advantages of such local topics are that students will write about issues in which they have some personal investment and may perhaps be able to gather information more easily. In addition, encouraging such topics works to prevent plagiarism, since canned essays are less likely to cover them. You might suggest that students return to this section when they begin their invention work.

Children Need to Play, Not Compete
Jessica Statsky

This essay treats a topic with which some students may have had personal experience: organized sports for children. The headnote invites them to reflect on their experience, and you might make this the subject of class discussion.

Connecting to Culture and Experience: Competition versus Cooperation

This activity focuses on Statsky's basic assumption about traditional American values. Once again, the discussion can take place in small groups or with the whole class. Students are invited to test her assumption against their own experience and observation. They are asked specifically to think about how the educational system deals with the ideas of cooperation and competition and also to examine their treatment in the media and advertising. The point is to get them to come up with specific instances to support one point of view or the other.

Analyzing Writing Strategies

1. Here we focus on the use of anecdotes to support a position. Students are likely to see that Statsky's anecdotes are effective because they dramatically make her points that fear of injury takes the enjoyment out of sports and that competitive sports often bring out the worst in adults. You might make Statsky's anecdotes the focus of a class discussion.

2. Statsky refers to as many as twelve authorities, including Dr. Tutko (paragraph 3), the mother of a Peewee Football player (paragraph 4), Rablovsky and several unidentified studies (paragraph 5), and so on. Since there are so many authorities cited, you might divide them among the students (working in pairs or small groups) and have them report their conclusions to the class.

Commentary: A Clear Position

This commentary treats an important aspect of one basic feature of this kind of writing: qualifying the position. Statsky is careful (some readers may think overly careful) to state the issue precisely. You might ask students to consider whether each of her distinctions is really needed. For example, she specifies noncontact as well as contact sports. This distinction would be important if someone argued that contact sports might be dangerous to children but that noncontact sports are not.

See the following exercise based on this reading in Chapter 11: Strategies for Arguing:

• Exercise 11.5 on using statistics

Considering Topics for Your Own Essay

Students will be surprised at how many controversial issues related to childhood and adolescence they can come up with. You might generate the list in a class brainstorming session and then invite students to choose a topic and discuss it with the other students who chose the same topic.

PURPOSE AND AUDIENCE

This section treats purpose and audience in position-paper writing. Purpose and audience are basic concepts for every type of writing, but they are essential for argumentation. The argumentative strategy that writers devise depends on how well they can anticipate their readers' assumptions and values and adjust their purpose to their particular audience. We identify a spectrum of purposes and audiences. You might ask students to try to infer the writers' aims and assumptions about readers from the selections in this chapter.

BASIC FEATURES: POSITION PAPERS

In this section we review the important characteristics of the position paper:

• A focused presentation of the issue
• A clear position
• Plausible reasons and convincing support
• Anticipating opposing positions and objections

As you move through the argumentative writing chapters, you might want to point out that many of the same features are considered essential.

GUIDE TO WRITING
Invention and Research

We recommend the following invention activities to help students analyze the issue and develop an argument for particular readers:

- Finding an issue to write about
- Exploring the issue
- Analyzing potential readers
- Testing your choice
- Developing your argument
- Anticipating readers' objections and questions
- Anticipating opposing positions
- Considering document design
- Defining your purpose for your readers
- Formulating a tentative thesis statement

Under the first heading, we propose a list of possible topics to get students thinking of issues in which they have an interest. Throughout the "Arguing a Position" Writing Guide, we encourage students to consider their purpose and audience, and we also emphasize the deliberative aspects of argumentation, asking students to explore all sides of the issue.

Testing Your Choice: A Collaborative Activity

This collaborative activity really serves as a further way for students to test their choice of topic. Students are asked to tell the others about the issue they have chosen to address in their essays. The task of briefly explaining an issue is not as simple as it may sound. To explain the issue, students need to have given it considerable thought and also to have some sense of how much their listeners know about it. If students find that their group members see the issue differently than they do, they may need to redefine it for the others, indicating why they see it as they do.

If the issue is one that the others in the group feel strongly about, they may wind up debating it. Although such a discussion could take up more time than your schedule allows, debating can be a very productive invention and critical thinking exercise.

Planning and Drafting

If you have students working in groups, you might give them an opportunity to discuss their goals and plans. You could have them bring a tentative outline to class to present to the group. The group members could then query the writer as to how certain elements of the outline embody the writer's purpose and expectations about readers. Students, for example, might ask the writer what made her decide on a particular sequence of reasons or why she chose to refute a particular argument. Explaining her plans might lead the writer to clarify or even modify them. The group could also help the writer consider other possibilities. Such a discussion could help the writer develop not only her thinking on the issue but also possibly a better sense of audience.

Critical Reading Guide

Students are likely to take lightly the request that they identify their purpose and audience for their readers. For example, they may assume that all they need to say about purpose is that they are trying to convince readers to accept their position. Since readers seldom adopt writers' positions completely, however, writers dealing with highly controversial issues usually have more limited—and realistic—aims. They might aim, for example, to get readers to accept certain arguments even if they won't accept the writer's conclusion. You might want to spend some time discussing purpose so that students can better prepare their readers.

Since position papers are difficult intellectually as well as rhetorically, you might want to organize more than one reading, focusing each time on different features. A first reading, for example, might focus on presentation of the issue and statement of the thesis, while further readings might focus on the points in the argument and their organization.

Revising

You might want to point out to students that the guides for the reader in the previous section and the plan for revising presented here all center on the basic features of position papers. The plan for revising leads them to identify problems having to do with the basic features in their drafts. The advice under Carrying Out Revisions is also organized by the basic features. The rationale for organizing all of this material around the basic features is that it gives students a way to focus their revision on one thing at a time.

Although the advice for solving problems is quite detailed, it is meant only to be suggestive. You might also remind students of how the writers they have read handled potential problems. If students have been working in groups, it might be profitable to have them discuss with their group members one or two of the problems with their drafts and their ideas for solving those problems. Getting students involved in actively discussing their drafts should encourage them to do some substantial revision.

Editing and Proofreading

This section provides an opportunity for students to focus on issues of grammar and style, and for you to address these issues within the context of their writing. You might set aside time in class for students to proofread and edit their own essays or exchange papers and proofread and edit each other's.

REFLECTING ON YOUR WRITING

As students complete their own projects, we ask them to reflect carefully on their experience with writing essays that take positions on controversial issues. Students are asked to reexamine the process of writing their own essays and to explain how they solved a particular problem.

RESPONDING TO ESSAYS TAKING A POSITION

You might expect to find problems like the ones listed below in student essays taking a position on a controversial issue.

Issue

- The issue the student is writing about is not really an issue—no one is debating it.
- The issue is not adequately described, or opposing views are not clearly explained.

Position

- The writer does not assert a position on the issue; the writer may waffle, agreeing with one side and then the other, but never take a stand.
- The writer merely reports opposing positions.
- The thesis is asserted too soon or too late.
- The key terms of the thesis do not seem appropriate and are not carried through the essay.

Argument

- It is difficult to see exactly why the writer takes the position; the reasons would be difficult or impossible to list.
- There is no explicitly cued, logical progression to the argument.
- The argument would be stronger if the points were arranged in a different order.
- Support is thin—relatively few examples, anecdotes, statistics, etc.
- The argument is adequately supported but seems flat, uncommitted, lacking surprises or insights, and likely to bore readers.
- The writer ignores readers—no objections or opposing arguments accommodated or refuted.

Tone

- The tone seems inappropriate to the writer's purpose and assumed readers.

PREPARING FOR CONFERENCES

If you hold conferences with your students on their drafts, you could have them prepare for the conference by filling in the form on the next page.

CHAPTER 6: PROPOSING A SOLUTION
THE WRITING ASSIGNMENT

Write an essay proposing a solution to a problem. Choose a problem faced by a community or group to which you belong, and address your proposal to either one or more members of the group or to outsiders who might help solve the problem.

The Nature of the Writing Assignment

Proposal writing reinforces the aim of argument as positive and constructive — to convince readers to solve a common problem in a particular way. This view of argumentation (sometimes called Rogerian because it is based on the work of psychologist Carl Rodgers) assumes that, to get readers to consider alternatives, it is necessary to reduce their sense of threat. Hence, argumentation becomes an effort not to defeat an opponent but to bridge differences by finding or creating common ground.

Learning to write a proposal directly engages students in learning to write for particular readers. For this reason, we have narrowed the scope of the writing task by asking students to propose solutions to problems plaguing communities or groups to which they belong. We want students to practice writing for particular readers whose interests and values they could imagine. In the Guide to Writing, we urge students to anticipate their readers' possible objections, foresee their alternative proposals, and figure out which reasons and evidence they would find more persuasive.

Since many proposals written in the workplace are collaborative, it would be a valuable experience for students to work through this assignment in collaboration with others. Small groups might work together to research a problem and solution and write individual essays, or a group might write a collaborative essay, with each student responsible for a specific section. You could limit them to problems on your campus. Or you might incorporate a service learning project into this assignment and send them out into the community to solve a local problem.

Special Problems of This Writing Assignment

Special difficulties students sometimes encounter as they write proposals involve topic choice and the need to establish the problem's existence and seriousness. Even though students are asked to write about a problem faced

PREPARING FOR A CONFERENCE: CHAPTER 5

Before the conference, write answers to the questions below. Bring your invention writing and first draft to the conference.

1. Which controversial issue are you writing about? How did you come to choose it? Why are people still debating it?

2. What is your position on the issue?

3. Who are your readers and how do you want to influence them?

4. For what reasons do you take this position? Be prepared to talk about their relation to each other, their sequence in your essay, and ways you might anticipate readers' objections to them.

5. What are you most pleased with in this draft? Be specific.

6. What specifically do you need to do next to revise your draft? List any problems you see in the draft or any that other readers have noticed. Say briefly how you might attempt to solve these problems. Use the back of this form for these notes. (If you have completed the text's Revising plan, bring it with you to the conference instead of answering this question.)

by a group to which they belong, they sometimes take on problems that are too abstract or complicated for them to handle effectively in a short time. It is understandable that students should want to solve some of the major problems we as a society face—such as the threat of terrorism, the lack of shelter for the homeless, or the deterioration of our industrial urban centers. As much as we do not want to discourage students from trying to understand these problems and even possibly contributing to their solution, we also do not want them to fail in their attempts to write successful proposals because their writing is too general. This chapter is designed to teach students how to gather the information they need to make their writing more specific.

A good proposal does two things: It defines a problem and argues for a particular solution. We have found that even the student who argues effectively for a solution may sometimes fail to establish that the problem exists and is serious. Defining the problem actually requires careful assessment of the rhetorical situation. The student must decide just how aware of the problem the readers are and how best to convince them that it is worthy of their attention and possibly their time and money as well.

Promising and Unpromising Topics

Choosing an appropriate topic is probably the hardest part of proposal writing. Some students know immediately what they want to write about, while others are at a loss. Perhaps the greatest stumbling block is abstractness. The more distant the problem is from the writer's personal experience, the harder it is to write about. That is why we urge students to choose a problem plaguing a community or group to which they belong. Even the most abstract problems can be treated in the context of a local group. Those concerned with broad educational problems, for example, might find evidence of the problem in their own high school or college. Those concerned with social and economic problems like homelessness and unemployment might look in their communities. To encourage students to localize abstract problems, you could have them each write down on a sheet of paper a national or international problem that concerns them. Each then passes his or her problem to another student, who then writes down a local, personal version of the problem. As a class, you could discuss the ways in which they've narrowed the topics. [Activity suggested by Joan Costello, Inver Hills Community College.]

Writing about a problem in a group to which they belong will also help students with the crucial task of analyzing their readers. They can more easily anticipate possible objections to their solutions and alternative solutions others might offer. They can also draw on common values, interests, and experience to establish the seriousness of the problem and argue for the feasibility of the proposed solution.

CHAPTER INTRODUCTION

Writing in Your Other Courses

Writing in the Community

Writing in the Workplace

These essay examples from college classes, the community, and the workplace all require analyzing a problem and proposing a solution to it. For all situations, an audience is specified. You will want to discuss with students that analyzing, researching, and explaining the problem are important steps for this writing purpose, but that they are all preliminary to and supportive of the main emphasis: the presentation of the solution.

Practice Proposing a Solution: A Collaborative Activity

By participating in this group activity so early in the process, long before they begin to consider their own topics and even before they discuss the chapter readings, students will be drawn surprisingly quickly into the complexities and possibilities of proposing solutions to problems. This activity has the benefits of preparing the students for the readings and anticipating the entire chapter. After about fifteen minutes, shift the students to the set of questions in the second part that ask them to step back and reflect together on the experience. After a few more minutes, shift the focus to whole-class discussion to share reflections on and reactions to the process of proposing solutions.

READINGS

These three readings should appeal to most of your students. All are on interesting and relevant topics, and all make lucid and well-reasoned proposals to solve serious problems.

Topics in Analysis Questions and Commentaries

This list can serve as a quick reference, indicating where each rhetorical concern is addressed. In class or in conference, you can use it to direct a student's attention to a particular area he or she needs to work on.

| *Ten Is a Crowd, So Change the Game*
Rob Ryder | Ryder's imaginative approach to a problem with the game of basketball may open up the possibility for students to choose topics that are compelling, but it is not as serious as some that might readily come to mind. In this intro- |

duction, we discuss his specific audience, readers of the *New York Times* sports section, and the ways in which his style suits this audience but would also be accessible to a wider audience.

Ryder, "Ten Is a Crowd, So Change the Game"	
Analyzing Writing Strategies 1. features of proposals 2. defining the problem and describing the solution	*Commentary: Anticipating Readers' Objections and Questions* anticipating objections and questions
Newman, "Dead-End Jobs: A Way Out"	
Analyzing Writing Strategies 1. defining the problem 2. alternative solutions	*Commentary: Describing the Proposed Solution* describing the solution
O'Malley, "More Testing, More Learning"	
Analyzing Writing Strategies 1. counterarguing 2. evaluating alternative solutions	*Commentary: Supporting the Proposed Solution* taking readers seriously organization

Connecting to Culture and Experience: Obsession with Watching Sports

Students should find this discussion interesting, as most will have some first-hand experience to draw from. You might assign this section as a small-group activity, perhaps with a journal entry as a follow-up exercise.

Analyzing Writing Strategies

1. This analysis exercise will familiarize students with the basic features of essays proposing solutions and help them become accustomed to evaluating proposals—others' and their own. They may have definite and differing views on the seriousness of the problem Ryder has chosen, depending on their own experience with and interest in basketball and other organized sports.

2. In this question we ask students to focus on Ryder's definition of the problem and description of the solution. Because his solution might be viewed as radical by some basketball fans, he devotes a paragraph to establishing his credentials as a player, coach, and film consultant. He also quotes experts in the field, two who endorse his proposal and one who voices the opposition. You might encourage students to speculate about why he includes the comment of the dissenting expert. This activity would work well as a small-group or whole-class discussion.

Commentary: Anticipating Readers' Objections and Questions

Ryder devotes a large section in his essay to anticipating the objections and questions of his audience, and in this commentary we focus on his approach to dealing with them. Students may not readily recognize the need to deal with opposing views in their own essays. They might assume, instead, that including their readers' objections and questions would weaken their own arguments. In fact, they may be surprised at Ryder's direct approach. Although students may not want to pose questions on behalf of their readers in their own essays, you might encourage them do so as part of the invention process, perhaps for a journal assignment. We end this commentary with specific advice about effectively handling opposing views.

Considering Topics for Your Own Essay

In this section, we suggest that students think imaginatively about possible topics—activities or enterprises that others might not see as needing solutions. You might ask students to work in small groups to discover topics, or you might assign this section as a journal entry during the invention process.

> *Dead-End Jobs:*
> *A Way Out*
> Katherine S. Newman

In the introduction to this essay, we stress Newman's credentials and her authority to propose a solution to this problem. We also point out that she wrote this proposal for specific readers who were in a position to carry out her proposal. You might take this opportunity to illustrate the advantages of addressing readers who can implement the solution.

Connecting to Culture and Experience: The Value of Routine, Repetitive Work

This activity, which works well with small groups, asks students to draw from their own experience to discuss low-paying, repetitive jobs. If your students are focusing on the thematic strand "work and career," this activity will be particularly useful.

Analyzing Writing Strategies

1. We focus here on the presentation of the problem. We ask students to first summarize the problem and then evaluate the effectiveness of the presentation for Newman's readers. You might consider using this question as a topic for a small-group activity.

2. This question asks students to describe the alternative solution that Newman refutes, to identify her reasons, and to evaluate her refutation. Since dealing with alternative solutions in their own essays may pose problems for students, you might want to work through this exercise with the whole class.

Commentary: Describing the Proposed Solution

This commentary focuses on one of the features of proposal writing—an adequately described solution. You might discuss Newman's description of her solution and this commentary with your students as they plan to describe their own solutions. We point out that she provides details about the consortium, defines it, and explains how it would function. Students may not immediately recognize that they will need to be so thorough in their own descriptions, and Newman's essay serves as a good model.

Considering Topics for Your Own Essay

Again, we ask students to generalize from their own experiences to identify problems that they might attempt to solve. We caution students to appeal to readers with similar experiences or with the ability to effect solutions. Students might work through this activity as a journal entry and then share their proposals with other students in small groups.

More Testing, More Learning Patrick O'Malley	This student essay shows students the advantages of careful invention, research, and revision. They should also note O'Malley's considerate treatment of readers' objections and alternative solutions.

He adds to his credibility by his responsible use of publications from educational psychology and his reference to a Harvard study.

Connecting to Culture and Experience: Experience with Frequent Exams

This activity connects students' personal experiences with the subject of the essay. As they discuss their own experiences with frequent exams, their interest in O'Malley's proposal will be heightened and they will be more receptive to the subsequent rhetorical focus in the questions for analysis. Once again, this discussion can take place in small groups or with the whole class.

Analyzing Writing Strategies

1. As we did in the Analyzing Writing Strategies section for Newman (question 2), we focus in this question and the next on dealing with opposing views. Here we ask students to analyze and evaluate O'Malley's counterarguments for his readers' likely objections. Students will note the strategies and resources O'Malley uses and evaluate their effectiveness, which will prepare them to evaluate their peers' counterarguments and to construct their own.

2. This question focuses on the strategies O'Malley uses to deal with alternative solutions. Keeping his readers in mind, students will evaluate the effectiveness of his counterarguments. You might want to use this ques-

tion, the preceding one, and question 2 in Newman as a small-group activity. Each group could work through one of the three questions and report the findings to the rest of the class.

Commentary: Supporting the Proposed Solution

This commentary accentuates the extreme care O'Malley takes with objections and alternative solutions. O'Malley did not merely speculate about his readers' responses to his solution; he also interviewed those directly involved to discover their objections, questions, and preferred solutions. Some instructors encourage or require their students to do interviews as part of the research for this essay. Useful information about conducting interviews is included in Chapter 12: Strategies for Field Research.

This section also presents the strengths of O'Malley's organization, of his careful weaving together of his argument and counterargument. You might spend time going over this outline with students when they begin to plan their own essays.

See the following exercises based on this reading in Chapter 11: Strategies for Arguing:

- Exercise 11.6 on analyzing the use of authorities
- Exercise 11.10 on accommodating readers

Considering Topics for Your Own Essay

This section asks students to write about a practice they have encountered in high school or college that could be refined or improved. You could generate some potential topics for it through whole-class brainstorming and then assign a brief rehearsal of a chosen topic as journal writing.

PURPOSE AND AUDIENCE

As we have suggested, proposal writing, perhaps more than any other kind of writing, requires sensitivity to readers and careful thought to purpose. Throughout the chapter, we discuss the role that argumentative strategy plays in realizing the writer's understanding of the rhetorical situation. Here we remind readers of some of the problems proposal writers encounter with their readers and the ways in which they might try to solve them.

BASIC FEATURES

Here we review the most important features of proposals:

- A well-defined problem
- An adequately described solution
- A convincing argument in support of the proposed solution

- An anticipation of readers' objections and questions
- An evaluation of alternative solutions

These are basically the same features discussed in Chapter 5: Arguing a Position, the only difference being the shift from issue and position to problem and solution.

GUIDE TO WRITING

Invention and Research

Here is a list of the invention activities:

- Finding a problem to write about
- Analyzing and defining the problem
- Identifying your readers
- Finding a tentative solution
- Defending your solution
- Testing your choice
- Offering reasons for your proposal
- Considering alternative solutions
- Doing research
- Considering document design
- Defining your purpose for your readers
- Formulating a tentative thesis statement

You might want to give students an overview of the invention activities and discuss how much time you expect them to spend on them. You could do the first part of the invention, listing problems, in class as whole-class brainstorming or in small groups, beginning with the problems the students have generated in the Considering Topics for Your Own Essay sections and moving to other problems the students can think of. Students will progress through the invention sequence at different rates, but you can help them stay on track by requiring that they reach a certain point by a certain class meeting. If you ask them to bring their invention-in-progress to every class meeting, you can ask them to read aloud from it to begin class discussion or to share certain sections with their peers in pairs or small groups.

Testing Your Choice: A Collaborative Activity

This activity will give your students the opportunity to rehearse their plans before an actual audience. By talking with one another in small groups, they will clarify the meanings they have created through the invention exercises. As group members discuss their essay plans, they should question one another about their intentions: "How will you convince readers that the problem is serious?" "Whom do you plan to address your proposal to?" They will also be able to offer suggestions: "Let me tell you one alternative solution I can think of. It would be to . . ." "You know, there's a group here in town working on that problem. It's called . . ."

Planning and Drafting

The purpose of this section is to help students move smoothly from invention to drafting. After students take time to review their invention writings, they should set some goals for their essays. If there is time, students could explain their goals to you in a brief conference, or they could explain them to one another in small groups. As students move into drafting, you can remind them to rely heavily on their invention for material; if they find that the invention work they've done is not providing them with enough material, they may need to do more invention writing.

Critical Reading Guide

Since we argue that proposal writing requires a strong sense of audience, getting comments on the draft is especially valuable. You might encourage readers in a draft workshop to pretend they are the readers addressed in the proposal. Role playing like this can be informative and fun. Having two or three students listen as the writer reads the draft aloud might enhance the fun. The listener/readers could discuss the proposal as if they were at a meeting to consider its merits.

Revising

We find it useful to emphasize to students the importance of rereading and considering their draft as a whole before contemplating specific revision changes. We know that successful writers take time to review their drafts from a global, holistic perspective prior to considering what modifications they will make. Some students resist this step; once they have secured feedback from their classmates, they want to proceed directly to revising their drafts. It would be an excellent use of class time to ask students to study their peers' comments, reread their drafts carefully, and compose a scratch outline while they are in the classroom. They can then discuss their revision plans in small groups with the students who listened to or read their drafts.

Editing and Proofreading

In this section, we suggest that students proofread their essays and edit for sentence-level errors. You might ask students to edit and proofread their essays outside of class, or you might want to address issues of mechanics and usage in class within the context of their own essays.

REFLECTING ON YOUR WRITING

Once students have completed their own essays proposing solutions, we ask them to reflect on what they have learned about this genre. Students are asked to reexamine the process of writing their own essays and to explain how they solved a particular problem.

RESPONDING TO ESSAYS PROPOSING SOLUTIONS

You might expect to find problems like the ones listed below in students' proposal essays.

Problem

- It is not clear to whom the proposal is being presented and what the writer expects readers to do about it.
- The problem is much too large or complex for the student writer to enter the debate on it authoritatively: poverty in America, terrorism.
- The problem is too insignificant or temporary to matter to readers: noise in the dorms, lack of school spirit, poorly stocked vending machines.
- The problem shifts in mid-essay to something different, usually a result of not framing the problem clearly enough in the beginning.

Alternative Solutions

- Alternative solutions are not presented, where there are obvious alternatives.
- The alternative solutions are represented unfairly.
- Alternative solutions are not effectively refuted or accommodated.

Proposed Solution

- The essay focuses on causes or effects of the problem rather than proposing a solution.
- The writer complains about the problem at length and only expresses a demand that it be solved, rather than presenting a feasible solution.
- The essay offers too many solutions, without arguing effectively for one, or for a two-pronged or three-pronged attack on the problem.
- The essay naively proposes an entirely inadequate solution to a large, complex problem, or the proposed solution does not seem workable (it may be frivolous, too complex, or costly).
- The essay does not argue effectively for the proposed solution. (The proposed solution may lack reasons or evidence, or there may be logical fallacies in the argument.)

- The essay ignores obvious or major obstacles or objections to the proposed solution.
- The solution doesn't match the problem (solving the problem of children's excessive TV watching by having teachers assign a weekly environmental project), or it proposes a solution which has been tried unsuccessfully in the past (without showing why it could work this time).

Tone

- The essay moralizes, editorializes, or rails about the problem, lecturing the reader.
- The essay denounces those seen as causing the problem.
- The essay seems confused or unclear about the problem; it lacks authority.

PREPARING FOR CONFERENCES

If you hold conferences with your students on their drafts, you could have them prepare for the conference by filling in the form on the following page.

CHAPTER 7: JUSTIFYING AN EVALUATION
THE WRITING ASSIGNMENT

Write an essay evaluating a particular subject. Examine your subject closely, and make a judgment about it. Argue for your judgment with reasons and support.

The Nature of the Writing Assignment

Evaluation essays are so well understood, their features so well established, that we can hold students to a standard of performance that may surprise them in its fullness and preciseness. The evaluation essay is the last in a series of three argumentative writing assignments in this book:

Chapter 5: Arguing a Position
Chapter 6: Proposing a Solution
Chapter 7: Justifying an Evaluation

Writing an evaluation requires students to carefully consider their reasons. Sometimes they must bring criteria to the surface, examining their appropriateness for the subject and readers. Students may also need to consider whether their criteria must be justified. Since writing an evaluation nearly always draws students into comparison or contrast, this chapter provides an opportunity to work seriously with students on this basic writing strategy.

PREPARING FOR A CONFERENCE: CHAPTER 6

Before the conference, write answers to the questions below. Bring your invention writing and first draft to the conference.

1. What problem are you trying to solve? Why is it significant? Who is affected by the problem, and how much do they know about it?

2. What solution are you proposing to solve the problem?

3. Who are your readers? (An individual, committee, group?) Be very specific in identifying your readers. What action do you want them to take?

4. Which of your reasons do you think would be most convincing to these readers? Briefly explain why. How have you anticipated readers' objections to your proposed solution? What else could you do?

5. What alternative solutions do you think your readers might be considering? How have you handled these alternatives? What else could you do?

6. What are you most pleased with in this draft? Be specific.

7. What specifically do you need to do next to revise your draft? List any problems you see in the draft or any problems pointed out by other readers. Say briefly how you might attempt to solve these problems. Use the back of this form for these notes. (If you have completed the text's Revising plan, bring it with you to the conference instead of answering this question.)

Special Problems of This Writing Assignment

This seems like a straightforward assignment: Say whether you like or dislike something, and then say why. It can nevertheless go wrong in many ways the first time student writers try it. Students may not be willing to assert firm judgments, or they may not understand that they need to define their judgments. In addition, because they are unaccustomed to being held to the rhetorical requirements of a specific writing situation, student writers may overlook the requirement to describe the subject for readers who are unfamiliar with it. They may also unwittingly merge or blur their reasons because they lack confidence in them.

These problems suggest that before you ask students to analyze each other's drafts, you may want to have the class discuss sample essays to see how the writers meet the rhetorical requirements of the assignment. Furthermore, the problems of the assignment make the evaluation a good choice for a double assignment in which you ask students immediately to do a second essay on a different subject. For the first essay, you could give them two or three choices of subjects, such as the same story or movie, and then they could choose their own subjects for the second essay.

Perhaps the biggest problem of all arises when students risk doing this assignment from memory. To support an argument, writers need specific details. A subject to be evaluated needs to be studied and restudied before and during invention and drafting. Students should not evaluate a movie unless they can see it two or three times, nor should they evaluate a novel unless they have time to reread it.

Promising and Unpromising Topics

The first step in the Invention and Research section for this chapter asks students to list possible subjects for their evaluation essays. We provide a list of general topic areas to get students started, a list drawn from our own experience with successful and unsuccessful topics. As you can see, we suggest a range of possible topic areas—including culture, written work, education, government, and leisure—that extends far beyond the few examples we have provided through the chapter readings. We also suggest subjects from the two thematic strands "identity and community" and "work and career."

Our experience has shown us that the most successful essays are those that draw heavily on the writer's interests and expertise. Students who express an avid interest in skateboarding often write fine essays on skateboard magazines, skateboard parks, or skateboard models. Not only are they familiar with the standards usually applied to that field of interest, but they are also able to make comparisons and contrasts to related subjects (for example, other skateboard magazines, parks, or models) with some ease. The topics themselves can be quite ambitious—we have had some remarkable essays evaluating such things as strategic nuclear arms treaties and UAW contracts—but they are successful only when the student has expertise in the topic. You should, by all means, encourage your students to draw on their own strengths, knowledge base, and interests when choosing topics.

By and large, students have the least amount of difficulty evaluating consumer products. Criteria are fairly easy to establish, the essays themselves are not difficult to structure, and comparisons can often be found in personal experience. Students, however, have a tendency to slip into a kind of Madison Avenue prose, uncritically touting the virtues of their chosen product and making claims of "comfort" or "style" that are unsupported by evidence. Personal taste often takes the place of more objective bases for evaluation in essays about consumer products. We discourage essays about consumer products; some instructors forbid them.

We are also wary of topics that try to evaluate abstract concepts such as "friendship" or "greed." Though it is theoretically possible to write such evaluations, it is extremely difficult to decide upon appropriate standards for judgment. Even more difficult is determining the kind of evidence that might be brought to bear on such a topic. Our students have occasionally written creditable essays evaluating "capitalism" or "democracy," but the key to their success seems to lie in the fact that these concepts can be illustrated by referring to specific examples of free market economics or democratic government.

Easily the most promising topics are discrete, tangible objects or events that can be revisited and analyzed—a story or novel, movie, musical recording, concert, play performance, essay in this book, magazine, restaurant, college program or service. Before drafting, students can revisit the subject, taking careful notes. They can revisit once again before revising, keeping the subject *present* throughout the writing process. The immediate presence of a subject makes it easier for a student to amass the evidence or examples required in a strong evaluation essay.

CHAPTER INTRODUCTION

Writing in Your Other Courses

Writing in the Community

Writing in the Workplace

This section provides examples of writing evaluations in college courses, in community publications, and on the job. For a journal assignment or in-class discussion, students might contribute other examples from their own experience. Students may be surprised to discover how frequently this type of writing occurs.

Practice Evaluating a Subject:
A Collaborative Activity

This group inquiry activity is designed to engage students in the most basic and yet most difficult aspect of evaluative writing: choosing appropriate criteria or standards for judgment. Notice that the activity has two parts. First, students discuss the criteria they would use for evaluating the subject they have chosen. Then they reflect on the process of choosing standards. The second part of the task will likely be new for them because few students—indeed, few people other than experts in a field—think about the standards by which they judge things. Normally, we just make judgments without thinking seriously about the values underlying our judgments. Through this group inquiry activity, you can lead students to recognize the importance of self-reflectiveness and critical analysis.

If students have difficulty coming up with reasons, you might advise them to think of a particular instance they are all familiar with and to consider how they would judge that. The group inquiry activity asks them to arrive ultimately at a consensus about the reasons, but not about the judgment. Because the process of consensus building often involves argument, they should expect to disagree, and they need to see how such disagreement can help them anticipate and handle the rhetorical situation in which they will be writing.

READINGS

One of the reading selections in this chapter deals with popular culture: David Ansen evaluates the film *The Phantom Menace*. Next, Kristine Potter reviews a Web site. Finally, Christine Romano evaluates the essay "Children Need to Play, Not Compete," a student essay by Jessica Statsky included in Chapter 5: Arguing a Position.

Topics in Analysis Questions and Commentaries

For your convenience as a quick reference, we list below the discourse topics addressed in each of the Analyzing Writing Strategies questions and in the Commentary. You might use this list in class or in conference to refer students to particular discourse features they need to review.

Star Wars:
The Phantom Movie
David Ansen

In this introduction, we point out that although Ansen is aware that he may not influence his readers with his review because of the popularity of the *Star Wars* movies, he nonetheless supports his judgment with specifics from the film. We ask students to note in particular the way in which he uses plot details as support.

Connecting to Culture and Experience: Stereotypes

This activity asks students both to identify film characters who are ethnic stereotypes and to discuss the validity of taking such stereotyping into consideration in evaluating a film. We suggest that students work in small groups, but you might follow up with a whole-class discussion or a brief writing assignment, such as a journal entry. If your students are following

Ansen, "Star Wars: The Phantom Movie"	
Analyzing Writing Strategies	*Commentary: Subject and Judgment*
1. features of evaluative essays	subject
2. reasons	judgment
Potter, "Asthma on the Web"	
Analyzing Writing Strategies	*Commentary: Reasons*
1. support	reasons
2. thesis statement	forecasting topic sentences
Romano, "'Children Need to Play, Not Compete' . . . An Evaluation"	
Analyzing Writing Strategies	*Commentary: Support and Counterargument*
1. reasons	quoting, paraphrasing, summarizing
2. criteria for judging arguments	counterargument

the thematic strand "identity and community," this activity will be particularly fruitful.

Analyzing Writing Strategies

1. This question asks students to measure Ansen's evaluation of the film against the criteria for this particular genre. We want to reiterate the basic features of an evaluation essay early in this assignment and give students practice in analyzing these features to prepare them for their own writing. You might have them write their answers and then share them with the whole class.

2. You might have students work in small groups or pairs to identify Ansen's reasons for his judgment of the film. As a class, you might then discuss how successful he is at defending his judgment.

Commentary: Subject and Judgment

This commentary focuses on the ways in which Ansen contextualizes his judgment, providing a brief history of the *Star Wars* series, identifying the actors, describing the characters, and relating the plot. This information prepares readers for his judgment that the film has not measured up to his expectations. We also point out that Ansen's thesis, in which he states his judgment, has two of the three qualities of a good thesis—it is clear and arguable—and that although he does not qualify his thesis, he does deal with aspects of the film that he finds commendable. You might discuss with students the advantages and disadvantages of this particular strategy. You might also refer students to Chapter 11: Strategies for Arguing, which includes a more lengthy discussion of the thesis.

Considering Topics for Your Own Essay

For this activity students will need to think about the criteria they might use to evaluate a particular film and why these criteria would be familiar to their readers. This will require them to analyze their own assumptions about their readers. We also stress the importance of knowing the subject of the evaluation thoroughly, of, for example, viewing the film several times. You might introduce this assignment by talking about different film genres and their characteristics and then ask students to complete the assignment as a journal entry.

| *Asthma on the Web* |
| Kristine Potter |

This evaluation, written by a college student, demonstrates how someone's personal interest can give rise to an essay that will engage a wide audience. In the introduction we ask students to reflect on Potter's criteria for evaluating a Web site and to determine whether the same standards apply to other methods of research. This essay and its ancillary material would fit nicely into a larger assignment in which students assess the usefulness of Internet sources.

Connecting to Culture and Experience: Responsibility

This section directs students to examine the issues of responsibility for and authority over one's personal health and well-being. You might begin this activity by asking students to write briefly on their personal experiences with these issues, and then ask them to work in small groups to share those experiences and views. You might follow up with a whole-class discussion.

Analyzing Writing Strategies

1. For this analysis question, students evaluate Potter's use of figures from a Web site. They might work in small groups to analyze her choices and explanations of the figures and decide what they would do differently. If possible, they should go to the Web site to get a firsthand view of Potter's choices.

2. Here we ask students to evaluate Potter's thesis statement according to specific criteria identified in Chapter 8: Strategies for Cueing Readers and Chapter 11: Strategies for Arguing. You might assign this question in conjunction with an activity in which they evaluate their own and each other's theses in pairs or in small groups.

Commentary: Reasons

This commentary focuses on Potter's reasons for supporting her evaluation and on the ways in which she helps her readers navigate through her essay. We provide a scratch outline that illustrates how her thesis introduces and forecasts her reasons; then we note her use of topic sentences to organize them. You might want to spend time discussing this commentary and Potter's organization when students begin to plan their own essays.

Considering Topics for Your Own Essay

In this section we suggest that students consider Web sites that they frequently use as topics for evaluation. If you meet your class in an electronic classroom or have access to a computer lab, you might want to allow your students time for this activity during class. They might initially work in pairs, and then you could conduct a follow-up brainstorming session with the entire class.

> *"Children Need to Play, Not Compete" by Jessica Statsky: An Evaluation*
> Christine Romano

This essay, written by a first-year college student, demonstrates how standards drawn from the *Concise Guide* may be used to evaluate a written text. The appeal of this approach to this assignment is that students will find standards readily acceptable to readers. In addition, this exercise should fix the standards firmly in their minds and ultimately enhance their ability to read critically and argue effectively. In this introduction we again stress the importance of considering the intended readers when evaluating.

Connecting to Culture and Experience: Team Sports and Community

This section provides students with another opportunity to explore the thematic strand "identity and community." Students might do this activity in small groups; then you could bring them together as a class to discuss their definitions of community.

Analyzing Writing Strategies

1. Keeping Romano's readers in mind, students are asked to evaluate the reasons that she gives to support her judgment of Statsky's essay. They need to apply one of the standards that Romano uses to evaluate Statsky's essay: appropriateness of the reasons for the readers. You might have students complete this assignment in small groups.

   Here is a possible scratch outline of Romano's essay:

   • Introduces Statsky's essay, summarizing her thesis (1)
   • States judgment of Statsky's essay, forecasting own reasons (2)

- Notes appropriate support (3)
- Points out believable support (4–6)
- Shows incompleteness: fails to support one reason (7)
- Shows incompleteness: fails to anticipate readers' questions (8)
- Shows incompleteness: fails to give examples of no-contact sports (9)
- Restates her judgment (10)

2. You might assign this question, which asks students to evaluate Romano's argument, as a journal entry. If students are writing their own evaluations of argumentative essays, this exercise will give them useful practice. Whatever their subjects, it will also prepare them to read both their peers' and their own essays with a critical eye.

Commentary: Support and Counterargument

This commentary highlights the use of textual evidence as support. We discuss quoting, paraphrasing, and summarizing—pointing out when each is appropriate or particularly effective. In addition, we provide examples, distinguishing between the original and paraphrased texts and between summarizing and paraphrasing. These examples also demonstrate appropriate parenthetical documentation. Students may have little experience using textual evidence, so you might want to spend time going over this section in class, especially if they will be writing essays evaluating written texts.

The commentary also discusses a type of counterargument that is often useful in evaluation essays, regardless of whether the overall evaluation is favorable or unfavorable—acknowledging the weaknesses as well as the strengths of the item or text that is being evaluated. By counterarguing in this way, writers can anticipate readers' questions and objections.

Considering Topics for Your Own Essay

This section suggests another subject for an essay, one that may appeal to students because the standards for evaluating could be adopted from the text. You could refer students to this section when they begin the Finding a Subject section of Invention and Research.

PURPOSE AND AUDIENCE

This section gives you an opportunity to focus class discussion on the concepts of purpose and audience as they pertain to the writing of evaluation essays. The writing situations that open the chapter, together with the illustrative academic assignments in the introduction, should suggest the range of situations in which evaluative essays may be written.

The Ansen essay exemplifies a special use of evaluation: to review instances of popular culture such as films and television programs. If you ask students about the purpose of reviewing cultural artifacts like these, most students will answer in market terms: to help consumers decide which film to see. Although that is undoubtedly the way that readers of newspapers and magazines typically use reviews, Ansen's essay attempts to do something more. In the Connecting to Culture and Experience sections we attempt to make students aware of the ideological underpinnings of the evaluations.

BASIC FEATURES: EVALUATIONS

This section summarizes what students have learned from analyzing the readings. We emphasize four basic features:

- A well-presented subject
- A clear, authoritative judgment
- Appropriate reasons and convincing support
- Effective counterargument

This discussion of basic features forms a bridge from the readings to the student's own writing. The same features reappear in the Invention and Research activities, in the Critical Reading Guide, and in the Revising section. You may want to refer students back to this summary if they have problems with a particular feature.·

GUIDE TO WRITING

Invention and Research

We recommend these activities to help students choose a subject, determine what they think about it, and develop a reasoned argument supporting their judgment for their particular readers:

- Finding a subject to write about
- Exploring the subject
- Analyzing potential readers
- Testing your choice
- Developing your argument
- Considering document design
- Defining your purpose for your readers
- Formulating a tentative thesis statement

You might want to spend class time brainstorming possible subjects for evaluation. You could, of course, assign the whole class the same subject—an evaluation of a short story, an essay from a chapter in this book, or a film you show on video. If you want to allow greater choice but also want to give students the benefit of collaborative learning, you could invite them to work together in small groups of three to five. These groups could discuss the subject they've chosen, debate their different judgments, and read each other's drafts. Some instructors have found it especially useful for students to write the essay collaboratively. If you are attracted by this idea, be sure to consider—in advance—how you will grade the essay. Collaborative projects of this kind can be very productive, but they require careful planning and sensitive guidance to make them work well for everyone.

Probably the most difficult invention activity is Developing Your Argument. Students tend to have two kinds of difficulty: identifying the standards underlying their judgment and finding evidence. You can address the first problem by having students (working together in pairs or small groups) explain to one another why they think the reasons are appropriate. If students are already working together on the same subject, the topic of what standards they are applying will probably come up. Even if students are not familiar with the particular subject, the writer could describe the subject as fitting into a general class of things (e.g., horror films) and then the group could discuss the question: What makes a horror film good?

The second difficulty—finding evidence—requires the writer to have ready access to the subject being evaluated. If it is a film, the videotape should be available for students to replay. Also, students need to develop a system of notetaking that allows them to refer specifically to the film (for example, by quoting or paraphrasing particular bits of dialogue).

Testing Your Choice: A Collaborative Activity

This group activity allows students to discover the needs and assumptions of their readers. Writers will present their subjects to other students, who will in turn point out gaps in the information provided and suggest standards with which to evaluate those subjects.

Planning and Drafting

This section offers advice on reviewing invention writings, setting goals, outlining, and drafting. You may want to spend some class time discussing the goals. Then refocus the basic features in terms of actions students can take, given their particular rhetorical situation, to present the subject effectively and make the argument understandable and convincing.

Critical Reading Guide

This guide to critical reading helps students analyze each other's drafts the way they analyzed the readings at the beginning of the chapter. Once again, all the basic features of evaluation essays are the center of attention. Students are specifically asked to look at these features in the context of the writer's audience and purpose.

Revising

This section urges students first to get an overview of their own essays and a sense of their problems before attempting to solve any single problem. We also encourage students to put off considering readers' critical comments until they have made their own assessments of their essays' strengths and weaknesses.

Editing and Proofreading

In this section, students are asked to find and correct sentence-level errors. You might ask students to edit and proofread their essays outside of class or in class under your supervision.

REFLECTING ON YOUR WRITING

As students complete their own evaluation essays, we ask them to reflect on what they have learned from the writing they've done in this genre. Students are asked to reexamine the process of writing their own essays and to explain how they solved a particular problem.

RESPONDING TO ESSAYS MAKING EVALUATIONS

You might expect your students' evaluation essays to have problems like the ones listed below.

Subject

- The subject is not within the limits set by your assignment (you assigned reviews of current movies and the student evaluated a fast-food place).
- The subject is too broad (jazz music rather than a particular jazz recording).
- The subject does not lend itself to evaluation (the homeless, cigarette smoking, school spirit).

Judgment

- The essay describes the subject or merely identifies its strong and weak points, but it does not express a clear judgment based on evidence.
- The judgment is overstated, without appropriate qualification or clarification.

Argument

- There is too much descriptive, historical, or biographical background distracting from the argument.
- The argument consists of a string of unsupported value judgments ("The acting was good. The directing was excellent. The cinematography was well done").
- There are too many reasons, or too few.

- The reasons seem arbitrary and inappropriate, not based on standards usually applied to a subject of that kind.
- The reasons are not organized logically.
- The reasons do not support the judgment.
- The essay fails to provide enough evidence about the subject to be convincing.
- The essay falls back on "advertising language" or PR style.
- Faulty or circular logic: Something is "good" because it is entertaining; something is "good" because it presents contemporary issues.
- Similarly, something is not necessarily "good" because it is "realistic," or "bad" because it is not. Conversely, something is not "good" simply because it is "unusual," "offbeat," or "strange" (e.g., rock stars).

PREPARING FOR CONFERENCES

If you hold conferences with your students on their drafts, you could have them prepare for the conference by filling in the form on the next page.

CHAPTER 8: STRATEGIES FOR CUEING READERS

Whereas Part One introduces the possibilities and constraints of various kinds of nonfiction prose, Part Two focuses on writing and research strategies. The opening chapter brings together several topics that are generally taught in isolation: thesis, paragraphing, and cohesion. We combine these topics in one chapter called Strategies for Cueing Readers because we want students to think of thesis statements, paragraphing, cohesive devices, and connectives as part of a signaling system that writers use to help readers read and comprehend their texts. In effect, these are strategies that writers use to establish and maintain focus in writing.

The chapter is divided into five sections:

Orienting Statements. To suggest how writers can provide a context so that readers will understand each succeeding sentence, we discuss thesis statements and forecasting statements.

Paragraphing. To indicate how writers can use paragraphing to help readers, we show how indention affects readers and also how writers can use topic-sentence strategies to orient readers.

Cohesive Devices. To show how writers can enhance coherence by connecting key words and phrases, we illustrate the following cohesive devices: pronoun reference, word repetition, synonyms, sentence-structure repetition, and collocation.

Connectives. To demonstrate how writers signal and identify connections for readers by linking ideas between sentences and paragraphs, we

PREPARING FOR A CONFERENCE: CHAPTER 7

Before the conference, write answers to the questions below. Bring your invention writing and first draft to the conference.

1. What have you chosen to evaluate? How did you decide on this subject? What is your judgment of it?

2. Who are your readers, and what can you assume they know and think about your subject? How, specifically, do you hope to influence their thinking through your essay?

3. List the reasons for your judgment. Be prepared to talk about their appropriateness, sequence, and relationship.

4. What are you most pleased with in this draft? Be specific.

5. What specifically do you need to do next to revise your draft? List any problems you see in the draft or ones others have pointed out. Say briefly how you might attempt to solve these problems. Use the back of this form for these notes. (If you have completed the text's Revising plan, bring it with you to the conference instead of answering this question.)

survey the following transition strategies: logical, temporal, and spatial relationships.

Headings and Subheadings. To show how writers can provide their readers with visual cues about the content and organization of a text, we discuss headings and subheadings.

We illustrate each of these strategies extensively with examples by professional writers. The exercises invite students to see how these cueing strategies work in longer pieces of discourse.

OVERVIEW OF THE EXERCISES

8.1   Analyze the thesis and key terms in Statsky's "Children Need to Play, Not Compete" (Chapter 5).

8.2   Analyze forecasting in Romano's "'Children Need to Play, Not Compete' by Jessica Statsky: An Evaluation" (Chapter 7).

8.3   Analyze paragraphing in O'Malley's "More Testing, More Learning" (Chapter 6).

8.4   Analyze topic-sentence strategies in Ansen's "*Star Wars:* The Phantom Movie" (Chapter 7).

8.5   Analyze topic sentences and transitions in Toufexis's "Love: The Right Chemistry" (Chapter 4).

8.6   Analyze topic sentences in your own essay.

8.7   Analyze cohesive devices in Leshner's "Why Shouldn't Society Treat Substance Abusers" (Chapter 5).

8.8   Analyze cohesive devices in your own essay.

8.9   Analyze connectives in Orenstein's "The Daily Grind: Lessons in the Hidden Curriculum" (Chapter 3).

8.10   Analyze connectives in your own essay.

8.11   Analyze the use of headings in Potera's "Internet Addiction" (Chapter 4).

8.12   Analyze the possibilities for headings in one of your own essays.

SUGGESTIONS FOR TEACHING THE EXERCISES

8.1   Analyze the thesis and key terms in Statsky's "Children Need to Play, Not Compete" (Chapter 5).

You can use this exercise to stress the function of the thesis as a cueing device. As a follow-up, students might examine the effectiveness of the key terms in their own or in their classmates' thesis statements and essays. In pairs, students could trade essays and work through the exercise. They might then use the responses from their classmates when they revise their own essays.

8.2   Analyze forecasting in Romano's "'Children Need to Play, Not Compete' by Jessica Statsky: An Evaluation" (Chapter 7).

Some students wonder whether giving a detailed preview is advisable since it gives so much away. You might use this opportunity to discuss when writers need to forecast and how much forecasting they need to give. But recognize that this writing problem usually involves a broader one—how explicit should a writer be? Many inexperienced writers are afraid of being too obvious when stating a thesis or forecasting an essay. They do not know what readers expect and what etiquette to follow.

8.3   Analyze paragraphing in O'Malley's "More Testing, More Learning" (Chapter 6).

You might assign this exercise at the point when students are drafting and revising their own essays. After working through the exercise, perhaps as a journal entry, students could repeat it using their own essays or a class-mate's. As with Exercise 8.1, students could use the feedback from this exercise to revise their paragraphs.

8.4   Analyze topic-sentence strategies in Ansen's "*Star Wars:* The Phantom Movie" (Chapter 7).

It might be helpful to assign this exercise as a small-group activity, asking each group to analyze one or two paragraphs and then report their findings to the class.

8.5   Analyze topic sentences and transitions in Toufexis's "Love: The Right Chemistry" (Chapter 4).

After students complete this exercise, for a journal entry or for home-work, you might want to discuss it with them. They may have different opinions about the effectiveness of Toufexis's topic sentences as transitions, and you can encourage them to justify their views. You might have students do Exercise 8.7 as a follow-up to this one.

8.6   Analyze topic sentences in your own essay.

Students will use what they learned about the topic sentence and its various functions in the previous three exercises to complete this activity. You might incorporate this exercise into an in-class workshop of their drafts as part of the revising process. Students may work independently, in pairs, or in small groups to analyze and evaluate their topic sentences. If they discover that topic sentences are either missing or ineffective, they can discuss ways to improve them with their peers or you.

8.7   Analyze cohesive devices in Leshner's "Why Shouldn't Society Treat Substance Abusers" (Chapter 5).

Students might find this easier to do if they work in small groups, each group looking for a different cohesive device. They also might find it easier to study cohesion within paragraphs. Students might repeat this exercise using sample student essays, perhaps from *Sticks and Stones*.

8.8   Analyze cohesive devices in your own essay.

This exercise might be assigned as part of the revision process. You might guide the students through it in class and ask them to continue analyzing cohesive devices in the rest of the paragraphs for homework. As a follow-up to this activity, students might add necessary, appropriate cohesive devices to their essays as they revise.

8.9   Analyze connectives in Orenstein's "The Daily Grind: Lessons in the Hidden Curriculum" (Chapter 3).

The purpose of this exercise is not simply to locate connectives; it is to examine how they help readers make sense of what they are reading. Students should probably work in groups on this exercise, and they might also be asked to supply some alternative connectives that Orenstein could have used.

8.10   Analyze connectives in your own essay.

Along with Exercises 8.6 and 8.8, this one is particularly effective when assigned during the revision process because students will immediately see the relevance of it to their own writing. Students might work individually, in pairs, or in small groups to analyze the connectives in their essays and then make any changes that their analysis suggests are necessary. This exercise, as well as the other two, might productively be repeated with different essays throughout the course.

8.11   Analyze the use of headings in Potera's "Internet Addiction" (Chapter 4).

This exercise can be used as an in-class activity, with students looking first at the headings and then reading Potera's text. As a class, have students discuss the initial impression they got from reading just the headings and whether their understanding changed as a result of reading the entire essay. You may also want to have students consider the visual impact of the headings in terms of how they contribute to the essay's interest level and organization. See whether students think the headings are appropriate and consistent in form.

8.12   Analyze the possibilities for headings in one of your own essays.

If the majority of your students have written one or more essays that incorporate headings, this can be an in-class activity; otherwise, it may work best as homework. In either case, after students have made or revisited their selections, you may wish to begin discussion by surveying the class to see which genres students most frequently chose as candidates for this type of visual cue, and asking them why they chose those genres. Then, working in pairs or small groups, have students exchange essays and review and comment on one another's ideas: Do the headings highlight the essay's organization? Are there any that might be placed more appropriately? Are the headings worded consistently, or are there ways these headings might be made more consistent with one another? If any students have included more than one level of heading, groups can discuss whether the text is detailed enough to support these divisions. Students may also want to suggest additional ideas for using visual cues.

CHAPTER 9: STRATEGIES FOR ALL-PURPOSE INVENTION

Because each writing-activity chapter in Part One has its own invention sequence, we do not discuss invention as a general topic early in our text. Instead, we engage students immediately in invention at the beginning of each Guide to Writing in Chapters 2 through 7.

In this chapter, we catalog the familiar all-purpose heuristics or strategies of invention and inquiry in two categories:

Mapping: These graphic means of recording discoveries and seeing connections include clustering, listing, and outlining.

Writing: The various ways to use writing itself to discover what one knows and needs to know include cubing, dialoguing, dramatizing, journals, looping, and questioning.

You can orient students to this chapter and let them use it whenever they want, or you can make specific assignments from it, helping students learn to use some of the strategies. All of the strategies can support writing activities in Part One and specific strategies are recommended in the Guides to Writing. For example, in the Guide to Writing in Chapter 2: Remembering Events, students *list, loop* (write and then stop to focus their thoughts), *write a dialogue,* and *outline.* In addition, as students revise and edit their essays, they might use activities in this chapter to explore their subjects further or to solve problems in their drafts.

CHAPTER 10: STRATEGIES FOR READING CRITICALLY

In this chapter, we present various ways of using writing to think critically about your reading. To illustrate these strategies, we refer throughout the chapter to a sample reading selection—an excerpt from Martin Luther King Jr.'s "Letter from Birmingham Jail," provided near the beginning of the chapter.

The strategies include annotating, taking inventory, outlining, paraphrasing, summarizing, synthesizing, contextualizing, exploring the significance of figurative language, looking for patterns of opposition, reflecting on challenges to your beliefs and values, evaluating the logic of an argument, recognizing emotional manipulation, and judging the writer's credibility.

As with the preceding chapter on invention strategies, you can introduce students to this chapter and encourage them to use it whenever they like, or you can make specific assignments from it. Some of these strategies, such as inventorying, evaluating the logic of an argument, and judging the writer's credibility, are integrated into the Guides to Writing in Part One and can support the reading that students do in that section of the text.

CHAPTER 11: STRATEGIES FOR ARGUING

This chapter complements Chapters 5–7, the text's writing activities that require explicit argumentation. Since Chapter 11 offers a comprehensive introduction to the basic strategies of argument, you could devote some time to it before introducing your first argument assignment from Part One. On the other hand, two chapters in Part One—Chapter 5: Arguing a Position and Chapter 6: Proposing a Solution—also provide comprehensive introductions to all the basic strategies of argument, but they introduce them in a full rhetorical context. Consequently, you might want to have students begin Chapter 5 or 6 and do work in Chapter 11 only to consolidate rhetorical concepts and argumentative strategies they are analyzing and practicing while working on a full essay.

Among the strategies in Chapter 10: Strategies for Reading Critically are three specifically designed for analyzing and evaluating argument: evaluating the logic of an argument, recognizing emotional manipulation, and judging the writer's credibility. Other critical reading strategies in Chapter 10 will be useful as well.

In this chapter, we introduce students to the following strategies of argument:

- Asserting a thesis
- Giving reasons and support (examples, statistics, authorities, anecdotes, and textual evidence)
- Counterarguing (acknowledging, accommodating, or refuting)

OVERVIEW OF THE EXERCISES

Since we assume students will be practicing (drafting, revising) these strategies as they write essays in Chapters 5–7, only a few exercises in this chapter ask them to practice a strategy. Instead, we ask them to analyze the strategies at work in the context of full essays in Part One.

11.1 Write an assertion.

11.2 Analyze the thesis in any essay in Chapters 5–7.

11.3　Analyze the thesis in your own essay.

11.4　Evaluate the use of examples in Statsky's "Children Need to Play, Not Compete" and Nelson's "Adventures in Equality" (both in Chapter 5).

11.5　Analyze the use of statistics in Leshner's "Why Shouldn't Society Treat Substance Abusers?" and Statsky's "Children Need to Play, Not Compete" (both in Chapter 5).

11.6　Analyze the use of authorities in Potera's "Internet Addiction" (Chapter 4) and O'Malley's "More Testing, More Learning" (Chapter 6).

11.7　Analyze the use of anecdote in Statsky's "Children Need to Play, Not Compete" (Chapter 5).

11.8　Analyze the use of evidence in Romano's " 'Children Need to Play, Not Compete,' by Jessica Statsky: An Evaluation" (Chapter 7).

11.9　Evaluate the acknowledgment of readers in Newman's "Dead-End Jobs: A Way Out" (Chapter 6).

11.10　Analyze the accommodation of readers in O'Malley's "More Testing, More Learning" (Chapter 6).

11.11　Analyze the use of refutation in Leshner's "Why Shouldn't Society Treat Substance Abusers?" (Chapter 5).

SUGGESTIONS FOR TEACHING THE EXERCISES

11.1　Write an assertion.

Writing an arguable, clear, and qualified assertion is often a more challenging task than inexperienced writers can imagine. They may have difficulty in understanding the challenge, much less learning to meet it confidently, unless you help them one-by-one with their assertions. An assertion must be arguable, that is, of consequence to some readers and to the writer. An assertion is not arguable if it derives solely from personal preference. Finally, an assertion is arguable — and workable as an essay's thesis — if the terms are clear and exact and if they will sustain the argument as its key terms, to be repeated in nearly every paragraph right through to the conclusion.

The notion of "workable" is very important, in our experience. Unfortunately, a writer does not know whether the key thesis terms are workable without drafting the essay. Writers can, however, test an assertion by projecting an essay's argument and direction. And that is what we would encourage students to do as you help them evaluate their assertions. They will need to have specific readers in mind for an assertion if they are to decide whether it is appropriately qualified.

We spend much time in class preparing for argumentative essays, going from student to student, discussing assertions, with the class contributing.

11.2   Analyze the thesis in any essay in Chapters 5–7.

The exercises here return students to full essays in Part One so that they can see how writers' strategies can be used purposefully and shaped for particular readers. This exercise asks students to evaluate the thesis in one of the essays in Chapters 5 through 7. You might divide the class into four groups, assigning an essay to each group. Each student could evaluate the thesis on his or her own, and then groups could take some time at the beginning of class to share results. However we posed the assignment, we would want to ensure that students understood how to find and evaluate a thesis.

11.3   Analyze the thesis in your own essay.

You might assign this exercise during the revising process. Students may work individually, but you might also ask them to work in pairs, analyzing each others' theses and then discussing possible ways to revise them.

11.4   Evaluate the use of examples in Statsky's "Children Need to Play, Not Compete" and Nelson's "Adventures in Equality" (both in Chapter 5).

11.5   Analyze the use of statistics in Leshner's "Why Shouldn't Society Treat Substance Abusers?" and Statsky's "Children Need to Play, Not Compete" (both in Chapter 5).

11.6   Analyze the use of authorities in Potera's "Internet Addiction" (Chapter 4) and O'Malley's "More Testing, More Learning" (Chapter 6).

11.7   Analyze the use of anecdote in Statsky's "Children Need to Play, Not Compete" (Chapter 5).

11.8   Analyze the use of evidence in Romano's "'Children Need to Play, Not Compete,' by Jessica Statsky: An Evaluation" (Chapter 7).

These five exercises ask students to analyze the ways writers give reasons and support. You might want to go over the essays with your students before assigning the exercises, perhaps asking them to write journal entries for them or to work in pairs or small groups. You might also combine the exercises for a class in which you look at several ways to support an argument; each group would work on a different exercise and then report their findings to the class.

11.9   Evaluate the acknowledgment of readers in Newman's "Dead-End Jobs: A Way Out" (Chapter 6).

11.10   Analyze the accommodation of readers in O'Malley's "More Testing, More Learning" (Chapter 6).

11.11   Analyze the use of refutation in Leshner's "Why Shouldn't Society Treat Substance Abusers?" (Chapter 5).

Each of these exercises enables students to observe how writers anticipate their readers' concerns. We are always surprised at how few students have ever *noticed* this strategy, though they have heard and read it countless times. Students seem never to have been asked to do it in their own writing. Since it is an easy and satisfying strategy to master, we give it special attention in our classes. In every Guide to Writing in Chapters 5–7, anticipating readers in various ways is a major invention activity.

CHAPTER 12: STRATEGIES FOR FIELD RESEARCH

This chapter introduces two essential techniques of field research: observing and interviewing. Observations and interviews are required for Chapter 3: Writing Profiles but may be used for other essays in Part One as well. Although field research is not likely to be as important in most first-year composition programs as library research, we urge you to introduce these techniques to your students. They will not only make students more observant but also heighten their sensitivity to readers' varying needs and interests. Field research will be central to the academic majors and careers of many students. It engages them in a basic form of inquiry in the social sciences.

OBSERVATIONS

This section is keyed to the Guide to Writing in Chapter 3: Writing Profiles. In that chapter we refer students to the advice given here on conducting observational visits.

We recommend that any observation include these stages: planning the visit, observing and taking notes, reflecting on your observation, writing up your notes, and preparing for follow-up visits.

Whereas reflecting on observations should follow directly after the observational visit when the experience is still fresh in the observer's mind, writing up the notes can wait until the observer has considered what impression the description should give.

To help your students read their own and each other's observational notes and write-ups analytically, here are critical reading guides they could use.

Reading Observational Notes with a Critical Eye

Even though notes are not finished writing, they are an interesting written artifact. They represent the immediate translation of firsthand experience into written language. They reveal what catches the observer's attention in a new scene. They are interesting for what they include and what they ignore, as well as for how they are patterned. Students reading each other's notes will see how someone else, faced with the same writing situation, recorded his or her experience.

1. What is centrally important about these notes? What general impression do they give you of the person, place, or activity being observed?

2. What is the single most surprising or incongruous detail in the notes? Try to explain why you find this detail so surprising.

3. Consider the notes as a collection of sensory images (sights, smells, sounds, tastes, and touches). Point to the single most evocative or suggestive image, and then briefly explain what feelings and associations this image evokes in you.

4. Try to imagine the notes accumulating on the page during the time the writer was observing the scene. What does the order of these notes tell you about the way the writer was looking at the scene?

Reading Observational Write-ups with a Critical Eye

Composing observational notes into a report or write-up can be considered real writing because a write-up assumes particular readers and aims to create a specific impression. Write-ups as part of the profile assignment in Chapter 3: Writing Profiles, however, do not serve as ends in themselves but as means to an end. In fact, the very process of writing up observational notes enables a writer to analyze and reorder them to reach a better understanding of how they might be useful in a profile.

1. What general impression of the place, person, or activity does this write-up give you? In one sentence, try to summarize your impression.

2. What order or pattern has the writer imposed on his or her observations? Are the details organized spatially, temporally, in groups, randomly, or some other way?

3. Where is the writer in relation to the subject? Does the writer use a moving vantage point, a stationary one, or a combination of the two? Does the writer move in close, remain at a distance from the subject, or shift perspectives?

4. What is the single most evocative image? Briefly explain what feelings or associations this image evokes in you.

5. Has anything you particularly liked in the notes been left out? Suggest where it could be included.

6. Are you left with any questions about the subject? List any information you would still like to have about this subject.

INTERVIEWS

Like the section on observations, this section on interviews is keyed to the Guide to Writing in Chapter 3: Writing Profiles. In that chapter, we urge students to study the advice offered here on conducting interviews. We recommend that students follow these steps: Set up and plan the interview, take notes during the interview, reflect on the interview immediately afterward, and write up the interview notes at a later time. We emphasize the need to plan an interview by writing questions, and we also discuss various kinds of questions to ask.

Here are guidelines for reading interview notes and write-ups. We urge you to offer these guides to your students to help them analyze their own and their classmates' interview material.

Reading Interview Notes with a Critical Eye

Like observational notes, interview notes are interesting to study in isolation and as raw material for an interview write-up. These guidelines assume that students have followed the suggestions for interviewing, written several questions in advance, and divided their notebook paper between Details and Impressions in the left-hand column and Information in the right.

First, read the interview notes and the writer's reflections directly following the interview. Then, briefly respond to these questions:

1. Compare the questions prepared in advance to the information received during the interview. Which of the questions were answered? What other questions seem to have been answered?

2. Study the information. Given the writer's reflections following the interview, identify what seems to you to be the most important bit of information the writer received in the interview.

3. Study the details and impressions. Identify one detail that is particularly evocative, helping you imagine the person and the scene. Then briefly explain what feelings and associations this detail evokes for you.

Reading Interview Write-ups with a Critical Eye

Interview write-ups are published in various forms in magazines and newspapers. In this chapter we encourage students to compose a write-up that is more than a mere compilation of quotations and details. The following guide was written to enable students to evaluate each other's interview write-ups.

1. What is your general impression of the person being interviewed? What details help you imagine the person? What else would you like to know about the person?

2. What particular angle of vision on the subject does this person give the writer? Do the person's comments raise any interesting new questions about the subject? Do they suggest any incongruities or surprises?

3. How much of the interview is quotation? Could the writer have paraphrased or summarized any of this quoted material without losing something of value?

4. Describe how the writer organized the quotations, paraphrases, summaries, descriptive details, and so forth. Is the description clumped together at the beginning, or is it interspersed with the other features? Advise the writer on possibilities for better integrating these features.

CHAPTER 13: STRATEGIES FOR LIBRARY AND INTERNET RESEARCH

This chapter and the next present first-year college students with all the information they need to do library and Internet research and to document a research paper. Knowing, however, is not the same as doing. We urge you to arrange a library tour and Internet orientation for your students, one that not only follows the steps in the search strategy but also gives students actual experience with many of the research materials introduced here — encyclopedias, bibliographies, card and online catalogs, indexes, abstracts, computer databases, and government publications.

We also urge you to have your students do some library and/or Internet research for several of their papers in your course. The only writing activities in Part One that do not invite formal research are the reflective essays — remembering events. Research could be used for every other assignment. You would not have to make any of these essays a major research project. Research need not make writing seem more difficult or more time-consuming but should be viewed as a strategy used routinely, like clustering or reading a draft critically.

This chapter shows students how to approach library research and carry out all the stages of a research project. Besides describing many types of library-research sources and opening up access to academic sources, the chapter identifies sources useful for researching current controversies (assignment for Chapter 5: Arguing a Position).

In addition to guiding students in their use of the library, this chapter introduces students to the Internet as a resource tool for research. To help students learn their way through the vast array of sources available online, consider conducting a "tour" of the Internet. Before students begin the online tour, it is best to assign Using the Internet for Research (see page 378) for them to read in advance. You can then go through each section in class while sitting at the computer, giving your students a hands-on experience. If you can, arrange to use an overhead projector that can display your computer screen. As you work through the section, students can get a look at various Web sites, learn what URLs and Web browsers are, and even watch as you use a search engine. To encourage your students to try electronic sources, Vicky Sarkisian of Marist College suggests that you use the material on the Internet in conjunction with one of the writing assignments that may involve research in Part One. Once they have defined their topics and begun the invention work, students would then be responsible for locating material using the World Wide Web. Stress that they should download and print their own material and learn to cite and document electronic sources properly. You might encourage them to create bookmarks for future reference.

Evaluating online text poses special problems. Instructors should start with traditional guidelines for evaluating text material and move from there (see Reading Sources with a Critical Eye). Because search engines prioritize information when they provide search results, you might do a model search with your students, noting the number of hits and the criteria the search engine uses for judging the sites. You should also point out to students that anyone with the knowledge and equipment can create a Web site and that it is important to deal with reputable sites such as those connected with libraries, museums, and universities.

As with any method of research, problems do arise when students use the Internet. Because hardware and software problems can be time-consuming, you should be knowledgeable about the Internet and willing to teach the system. Also, make sure that technical support is available before beginning any Internet work with your students. In addition to problems with determining the credibility and reliability of sources, students need to be warned about plagiarizing online sources. Because information is so readily available, you will need to thoroughly cover your school's plagiarism policy and stress the importance of documenting sources. See *The St. Martin's Guide* Web site <http://www.bedfordstmartins.com/theguide> for more on evaluating Internet sources.

Finally, be flexible and be prepared with an alternate plan: If the Internet is down or unavailable, it can derail your plans for a class or delay your students' research. However, the Internet is a valuable tool for learning, and it can help students greatly if they learn to use it accurately and carefully.

CHAPTER 14: STRATEGIES FOR USING AND ACKNOWLEDGING SOURCES

The first of the two sections in this chapter, Using Sources, teaches students how to integrate source material into their writing. Next, Acknowledging Sources surveys MLA and APA documentation style and format.

In this chapter we briefly discuss plagiarism to clarify what is meant by the term and to bring into the open some of the reasons why writers plagiarize. We define *plagiarism* broadly as the "unacknowledged use of another's words, ideas, or information." You may wish to discuss these issues in class, and you will probably also wish to inform students of your own and your institution's policy regarding plagiarism.

Most students who plagiarize, we assume, do not understand that the acknowledged use of other people's ideas, information, and even words is not only acceptable but expected of educated people. For this reason, if for no other, we believe students should routinely be asked to consult sources when they write. If this is done, students will begin to understand that, for the most part, academic writing is a dialogue between the writer and other writers on a given subject.

We also assume that plagiarism is in many cases simply evidence of students' unfamiliarity with academic conventions in our culture. They plagiarize because they do not know how to integrate source material into their own writing. Using Sources surveys various acceptable methods of quoting, paraphrasing, and summarizing source material. In many cases, we use illustrations from essays in Part One so that students can see how these strategies are used in the context of a whole selection. You might take some class time to discuss these strategies and suggest others students might add to their repertoire.

Appendix

A Selected Bibliography in Rhetoric and Composition

HISTORIES OF RHETORIC AND THE TEACHING OF WRITING

Applebee, Arthur N. *Tradition and Reform in the Teaching of English: A History.* Urbana: NCTE, 1974.

Bender, John, and David E. Wellbery. *The Ends of Rhetoric: History, Theory, Practice.* Stanford: Stanford UP, 1990.

Berlin, James A. *Rhetoric and Reality: Writing Instruction in American Colleges, 1900–1985.* Carbondale: Southern Illinois UP, 1987.

———. *Writing Instruction in Nineteenth Century American Colleges.* Carbondale: Southern Illinois UP, 1984.

Bizzell, Patricia, and Bruce Herzberg, eds. *The Rhetorical Tradition: Readings from Classical Times to the Present.* Boston: Bedford/St. Martin's, 2001.

Brereton, John, ed. *Traditions of Inquiry.* New York: Oxford UP, 1985.

Connors, Robert J. "The Rise and Fall of the Modes of Discourse." *CCC* 32 (1981): 444–63.

Connors, Robert J., Lisa S. Ede, and Andrea Lunsford, eds. *Essays on Classical Rhetoric and Modern Discourse.* Carbondale: Southern Illinois UP, 1984.

Corbett, Edward P. J., James L. Golden, and Goodwin F. Berquist, eds. *Essays on the Rhetoric of the Western World.* Dubuque: Kendall/Hunt, 1990.

138

Crowley, Sharon. *The Methodical Memory: Invention in Current-Traditional Rhetoric*. Carbondale: Southern Illinois UP, 1990.

———. *Ancient Rhetorics for Contemporary Students*. New York: Macmillan, 1994.

Ede, Lisa, ed. *On Writing Research: The Braddock Essays, 1975–1998*. Boston: Bedford/St. Martin's, 1999.

Halloran, S. Michael. "Rhetoric in the American College Curriculum: The Decline of Public Discourse." *PRE/TEXT* 3 (Fall 1983).

Horner, Winifred Bryan, ed. *The Present State of Scholarship in Historical and Contemporary Rhetoric*. Columbia: U of Missouri P, 1983.

Jarratt, Susan. *The Return of the Sophists: Classical Rhetoric Refigured*. Carbondale: Southern Illinois UP, 1991.

Johnson, Nan. *Nineteenth-Century Rhetoric: Theory and Practice in North America*. Carbondale: Southern Illinois UP, 1991.

Kennedy, George A. *Classical Rhetoric and Its Christian and Secular Tradition from Ancient to Modern Times*. Chapel Hill: U of North Carolina P, 1980.

Murphy, James J., ed. *The Rhetorical Tradition and Modern Writing*. New York: MLA, 1982.

———. *A Short History of Writing Instruction from Ancient Greece to Twentieth Century America*. Davis: Hermagoras, 1990.

Phelps, Louise Wetherbee. *Composition as a Human Science: Contribution to the Self-Understanding of a Discipline*. New York: Oxford UP, 1988.

Royster, Jacqueline Jones. "Perspectives on the Intellectual Tradition of Black Women Writers." *The Right to Literacy*. Ed. Andrea Lunsford et al. New York: MLA, 1990.

Swearington, C. Jan. *Rhetoric and Irony: Western Literacy and Western Lies*. New York: Oxford UP, 1991.

Welch, Kathleen E. *The Contemporary Reception of Classical Rhetoric: Appropriations of Ancient Discourse*. Hillsdale: Erlbaum, 1990.

MODERN AND POSTMODERN RHETORIC AND DISCOURSE THEORY

Aronowitz, Stanley, and Henry A. Giroux. *Postmodern Education: Politics, Culture, and Social Criticism*. Minneapolis: U of Minnesota P, 1991.

Atkins, C. Douglas, and Michael L. Johnson, eds. *Writing and Reading Differently: Deconstruction and the Teaching of Composition and Literature*. Lawrence: UP of Kansas, 1985.

Beale, Walter H. *A Pragmatic Theory of Rhetoric*. Carbondale: Southern Illinois UP, 1987.

Belanoff, Pat, Peter Elbow, and Sheryl I. Fontaine, eds. *Nothing Begins with N: New Investigations of Freewriting*. Carbondale: Southern Illinois UP, 1991.

Berthoff, Ann. *The Making of Meaning: Metaphors, Models, and Maxims for Writing Teachers*. Portsmouth: Heinemann, Boynton/Cook, 1981.

Bitzer, Lloyd F. "The Rhetorical Situation." *Philosophy and Rhetoric* 1 (Winter 1968): 1–14.

Bizzell, Patricia. *Academic Discourse and Critical Consciousness*. Pittsburgh: U of Pittsburgh P, 1992.

Britton, James, et al. *The Development of Writing Abilities (11–18)*. London: Macmillan, 1975.

Bullock, Richard, and John Trimbur, eds. *The Politics of Writing Instruction: Postsecondary*. Portsmouth: Heinemann, Boynton/Cook, 1991.

Clark, Gregory. *Dialogue, Dialectic, and Conversation: A Social Perspective on the Function of Writing*. Carbondale: Southern Illinois UP, 1990.

Crusius, Timothy W. *Discourse: A Critique and Synthesis of Major Theories*. New York: MLA, 1989.

Elbow, Peter. *Embracing Contraries: Explorations in Learning and Teaching*. New York: Oxford UP, 1986.

———. *What Is English?* New York: MLA, 1990.

Emig, Janet. *The Web of Meaning: Essays on Writing, Teaching, Learning, and Thinking*. Ed. Dixie Goswami and Maureen Butler. Portsmouth: Heinemann, Boynton/Cook, 1983.

Faigley, Lester. *Fragments of Rationality: Postmodernity and the Subject of Composition*. Pittsburgh: U of Pittsburgh P, 1992.

Freedman, Aviva, and Ian Pringle, eds. *Reinventing the Rhetorical Tradition*. Urbana: NCTE, 1980.

Giroux, Henry A. *Postmodernism, Feminism, and Cultural Politics: Redrawing Educational Boundaries*. Albany: SUNY P, 1991.

Kinneavy, James L. *A Theory of Discourse*. New York: Norton, 1980.

Lindemann, Erika, and Gary Tate, eds. *An Introduction to Composition Studies*. New York: Oxford UP, 1991.

Macdonnell, Diane. *Theories of Discourse: An Introduction*. Oxford: Basil Blackwell, 1986.

Miller, Susan. *Rescuing the Subject: A Critical Introduction to Rhetoric and the Writer*. Carbondale: Southern Illinois UP, 1989.

———. *Textual Carnivals: The Politics of Composition*. Carbondale: Southern Illinois UP, 1991.

Moffett, James. *Teaching the Universe of Discourse*. Boston: Houghton, 1968.

Perelman, Chaim. *The Realm of Rhetoric*. Trans. William Kluback. Notre Dame: U of Notre Dame P, 1977.

Schilb, John, and Patricia Harkin, eds. *Contending with Words: Composition and Rhetoric in a Postmodern Age*. New York: MLA, 1991.

Secor, Marie, and Davida Charney, eds. *Constructing Rhetorical Education*. Carbondale: Southern Illinois UP, 1992.

Toulmin, Stephen. *The Uses of Argument*. New York: Cambridge UP, 1964.

WRITING AS A PROCESS

Emig, Janet. *The Composing Processes of Twelfth Graders*. Urbana: NCTE, 1971.

Faigley, Lester. "Competing Theories of Process: A Critique and a Proposal." *CE* 48 (1986): 527–42.

Flower, Linda, and John R. Hayes. "Problem-Solving Strategies and the Writing Process." *CE* 49 (1977): 19–37.

Flower, Linda, et al. "Detection, Diagnosis, and the Strategies of Revision." *CCC* 37 (1986): 16–55.

Gregg, L. W., and E. R. Steinberg, eds. *Cognitive Processes in Writing.* Hillsdale: Erlbaum, 1980.

LeFevre, Karen Burke. *Invention as a Social Act.* Carbondale: Southern Illinois UP, 1987.

Murray, Donald M. "Writing as Process: How Writing Finds Its Own Meaning." *Eight Approaches to Teaching Composition.* Ed. Timothy R. Donovan and Ben W. McClelland. Urbana: NCTE, 1980.

Nystrand, Martin, ed. *What Writers Know: The Language, Process, and Structure of Written Discourse.* New York: Academic P, 1982.

Rose, Mike, ed. *When a Writer Can't Write: Studies in Writer's Block and Other Composing-Process Problems.* New York: Guilford, 1985.

Sommers, Nancy. "Revision Strategies of Student Writers and Experienced Adult Writers." *CCC* 31 (1980): 378–88.

Sudol, Ronald A., ed. *Revising.* Urbana: NCTE, 1982.

COMPUTERS AND COMPOSITION

Cooper, Marilyn M., and Cynthia L. Selfe. "Computer Conferences and Learning: Authority, Resistance, and Internally Persuasive Discourse." *CE* 52 (1990): 847–69.

Hawisher, Gail E., and Cynthia L. Selfe. *Critical Perspectives on Computers and Composition Instruction.* New York: Teachers College P, 1989.

Holdstein, Deborah H., and Cynthia L. Selfe, eds. *Computers and Writing: Theory, Research, Practice.* New York: MLA, 1990.

Selfe, Cynthia L., and Susan Hilligoss, eds. *Literacy and Computers: The Complications of Teaching and Learning with Technology.* New York: MLA, 1994.

COLLABORATIVE LEARNING

Brooke, Robert E. *Writing and Sense of Self: Identity Negotiation in Writing Workshops.* Urbana: NCTE, 1991.

Bruffee, Kenneth A. "Collaborative Learning and the 'Conversation of Mankind.'" *CE* 46 (1984): 635–52.

———. *Collaborative Learning: Higher Education, Interdependence, and the Authority of Knowledge.* Baltimore: Johns Hopkins UP, 1993.

Gere, Ann. *Writing Groups: History, Theory, and Implications.* Carbondale: Southern Illinois UP, 1987.

Golub, Jeff, ed. *Focus on Collaborative Learning.* Urbana: NCTE, 1988.

Haring-Smith, Tori. *Writing Together: Collaborative Learning in the Writing Classroom.* New York: HarperCollins, 1994.

Lunsford, Andrea, and Lisa Ede. *Singular Texts/Plural Authors: Perspectives on Collaborative Writing.* Carbondale: Southern Illinois UP, 1990.

METACOGNITION, READING, AND GENRE THEORY

Bereiter, Carl, and Marlene Scardamalia. *Psychology of Written Composition*. Hillsdale: Erlbaum, 1987.

Brown, Ann L. "Metacognitive Development and Reading." *Theoretical Issues in Reading Comprehension*. Ed. Bertram Bruce et al. Hillsdale: Erlbaum, 1980.

Cope, Bill, and Mary Kalantzis, eds. *The Powers of Literacy: A Genre Approach to Teaching Writing*. Pittsburgh: U of Pittsburgh P, 1993.

Dillon, George L. *Constructing Texts*. Bloomington: Indiana UP, 1981.

Freedman, Aviva. "Show and Tell? The Role of Explicit Teaching in the Learning of New Genres." *RTE* 27.3 (Oct. 1993): 222–51.

———. "Situating Genre: A Rejoinder." *RTE* 27:3 (1993): 272–81.

Halliday, M. A. K., and Ruqaiya Hasan. *Cohesion in English*. London: Longman, 1976.

Kinsch, Walter. "The Role of Strategies in Reading and Writing." *Forum* III 67 (1982).

Kress, Gunther. "Genre as Social Process." *The Powers of Literacy: A Genre Approach to Teaching Writing*. Ed. Bill Cope and Mary Kalantzis. Pittsburgh: U of Pittsburgh P, 1993.

Miller, Carolyn. "Genre as Social Action." *Quarterly Journal of Speech* 70 (1984): 151–67.

Newkirk, Thomas, ed. *Only Connect: Uniting Reading and Writing*. Portsmouth: Heinemann, Boynton/Cook, 1986.

Petersen, Bruce T., ed. *Convergences: Transactions in Reading and Writing*. Urbana: NCTE, 1986.

Pianko, Sharon. "Reflection: A Critical Component of the Composing Process." *CCC* 30 (1979): 275–85.

Schank, R., and Abelson, R. *Scripts, Plans, Goals, and Understanding*. Hillsdale: Erlbaum, 1977.

Slevin, James F. "Interpreting and Composing: The Many Resources of Kind." *The Writer's Mind*. Ed. Janice Hays et al. Urbana: NCTE, 1983.

Williams, Joseph M., and Gregory G. Colomb. "The Case for Explicit Teaching: Why What You Don't Know Won't Help You." *RTE* 27.3 (1993): 252–64.

WRITING IN THE DISCIPLINES

Bartholomae, David. "Inventing the University." *When a Writer Can't Write*. Ed. Mike Rose. New York: Guilford P, 1985.

Bazerman, Charles. *Shaping Written Knowledge*. Madison: U of Wisconsin P, 1988.

Bazerman, Charles, and James Paradis. *Textual Dynamics of the Professions: Historical and Contemporary Studies of Writing in Professional Communities*. Madison: U of Wisconsin P, 1991.

Bullock, Richard. *The St. Martin's Guide to Teaching Writing in the Disciplines*. Boston: Bedford, 1999.

Fulwiler, Toby, and Al Young, eds. *Programs That Work: Writing across the Curriculum*. Portsmouth: Heinemann, Boynton/Cook, 1990.

Gere, Anne Ruggles, ed. *Roots in the Sawdust: Writing to Learn in the Disciplines.* Urbana: NCTE, 1985.

Herrington, Anne, and Charles Moran. *Writing, Teaching, and Learning in the Disciplines.* New York: MLA, 1992.

Howard, Rebecca Moore, and Sandra Jamieson. *The Bedford Guide to Teaching Writing in the Disciplines.* Boston: Bedford, 1995.

MacDonald, Susan Peck. *Professional Academic Writing in the Humanities and Social Sciences.* Carbondale: Southern Illinois UP, 1994.

Maimon, Elaine P. "Collaborative Learning and Writing across the Curriculum." *WPA* 9 (1986): 9–15.

Russell, David R. *Writing in the Academic Disciplines, 1870–1990.* Carbondale: Southern Illinois UP, 1991.

Walvoord, Barbara, and Lucille McCarthy, eds. *Thinking and Writing in College.* Urbana: NCTE, 1990.

GENDER, CLASS, ETHNICITY

Annas, Pamela J. "Style as Politics: A Feminist Approach to Teaching of Writing." *CE* 47 (1985): 369–71.

Ashton-Jones, Evelyn, and D. Thomas. "Composition, Collaboration, and Women's Ways of Knowing." *Journal of Advanced Composition* 10 (1990): 275–92.

Belenky, Mary Field, et al. *Women's Ways of Knowing: The Development of Self, Voice, and Mind.* New York: Basic Books, 1986.

Caywood, Cynthia L., and Gillian R. Overing. *Teaching Writing: Pedagogy, Gender, and Equity.* Albany: SUNY P, 1987.

Eichhorn, Jill, et al. "A Symposium on Feminist Experiences in the Composition Classroom." *CCC* 43 (1992): 297–322.

Flynn, Elizabeth A., and Patrocinio Schwickart, eds. *Gender and Reading: Essays on Readers, Texts and Contexts.* Baltimore: Johns Hopkins UP, 1986.

Fontaine, Sheryl, and Susan Hunter, eds. *Writing Ourselves into the Story: Unheard Voices from Composition Studies.* Carbondale: Southern Illinois UP, 1993.

Greco, Norma. "Critical Literacy and Community Service: Reading and Writing the World." *English Journal* 81 (1992): 83–85.

Heath, Shirley Brice. *Ways with Words: Language, Life, and Work in Communities and Classrooms.* Cambridge: Cambridge UP, 1983.

Hill, Carolyn Eriksen. *Writing from the Margins: Power and Pedagogy for Teachers of Composition.* New York: Oxford UP, 1990.

Langer, Judith A., ed. *Language, Literacy, and Culture: Issues of Society and Schooling.* Norwood: Ablex Publishing, 1987.

McCracken, Nancy Mellin, and Bruce C. Appleby. *Gender Issues in the Teaching of English.* Portsmouth: Heinemann, Boynton/Cook, 1992.

McQuade, Donald A., ed. *The Territory of Language: Linguistics, Stylistics, and the Teaching of Composition.* Carbondale: Southern Illinois UP, 1986.

Rose, Mike. *Lives on the Boundary: The Struggles and Achievements of America's Underprepared.* London: Collier-Macmillan, 1989.

Rubin, Donnalee. *Gender Influences: Reading Student Texts.* Carbondale: Southern Illinois UP, 1993.

Shaughnessy, Mina. *Errors and Expectations.* New York: Oxford UP, 1977.

Smitherman-Donaldson, Ginevra, and Teun A. van Dijk, eds. *Discourse and Discrimination.* Detroit: Wayne State UP, 1988.

RESPONDING TO AND EVALUATING STUDENT WRITING

Anson, Cris M. *Writing and Response: Theory, Practice, and Research.* Urbana: NCTE, 1989.

Belanoff, Pat, and Marcia Dickson. *Portfolios: Process and Product.* Portsmouth: Heinemann, Boynton/Cook, 1991.

Black, Laurel, et al. *New Directions in Portfolio Assessment.* Portsmouth: Heinemann, Boynton/Cook, 1994.

Cooper, Charles, and Lee Odell, eds. *Evaluating Writing,* 2nd ed. Urbana: NCTE, 1997.

Faigley, Lester, et al. *Assessing Writers' Knowledge and Processes of Composing.* Norwood: Ablex, 1985.

Freedman, Sarah W. *Response to Student Writing.* Urbana: NCTE Research Report No. 23, 1987.

Greenberg, K. L., et al., eds. *Writing Assessment: Issues and Strategies.* New York: Longman, 1986.

Horvath, Brooke K. "The Components of Written Response: A Practical Synthesis of Current Views." *Rhetoric Review* 2 (Jan. 1985): 136–56.

Williams, Joseph M. "The Phenomenology of Error." *CCC* 32 (1991): 152–68.

COMMUNITY SERVICE LEARNING

Adler-Kassner, Linda, Robert Crooks, and Ann Watters. "Service-Learning and Composition at the Crossroads." *Writing the Community: Concepts and Models for Service-Learning in Composition.* Washington: American Association for Higher Education/NCTE, 1997.

Bacon, Nora. "Community Service Writing: Problems, Challenges, Questions." *Writing the Community: Concepts and Models for Service-Learning in Composition.* Ed. Robert Crooks, Linda Adler-Kassner, and Ann Watters. Washington: American Association for Higher Education/NCTE, 1997.

Gere, Anne Ruggles, and Jennifer Sinor. "Composing Service-Learning." *Writing Instructor* 16:2 (1997): 53–64.

Heilker, Paul. "Rhetoric Made Real: Civic Discourse and Writing beyond the Curriculum." *Writing the Community: Concepts and Models for Service-Learning in Composition.* Ed. Robert Crooks, Linda Adler-Kassner, and Ann Watters. Washington: American Association for Higher Education/NCTE, 1997.

Herzberg, Bruce. "Community Service and Critical Teaching." *CCC* (1994): 307–19.

SUBMITTING PAPERS FOR PUBLICATION

TO STUDENTS AND INSTRUCTORS

We hope that we'll be able to include essays from more colleges and universities in the next edition of *Axelrod & Cooper's Concise Guide to Writing* and our accompanying anthology, *Sticks and Stones and other student essays.* Please let us see essays written using the *Concise Guide* you'd like us to consider. Send them with this Paper Submission Form and the Agreement Form on the back to *Concise Guide,* Bedford/St. Martin's, 33 Irving Place, New York, NY 10003.

PAPER SUBMISSION FORM

Instructor's name _____

School _____

Address _____

Department _____

Student's name _____

Course _____

Writing activity the paper represents _____

This writing activity appears in chapter(s) _____
of *Axelrod & Cooper's Concise Guide to Writing*

AGREEMENT FORM

I hereby transfer to Bedford/St. Martin's all rights to my essay,

(tentative title), subject to final editing by the publisher. These rights include copyright and all other rights of publication and reproduction. I guarantee that this essay is wholly my original work, and that I have not granted rights to it to anyone else.

Student's signature: X _____

Please type

Name: _____

Address: _____

_____

_____

Phone: _____

Please indicate the reader or publication source you assumed for your essay:

_____

Write a few sentences about the purpose or purposes of your essay. What did you hope to achieve with your reader? _____

_____

_____

_____

_____

_____

_____

Bedford/St. Martin's representative: _____